'OTHERS' IS NOT A RACE

Melissa De Silva was ⎡   ⎤ in the
power of stories to fo ⎢   ⎥ ihabit
(momentarily) other liv ⎢      ⎥ what
it means to be human. ⎢   ⎥ novel
and exploring the possib ⎣   ⎦ .....iig as a storytelling
platform to explore the themes she is most drawn to: cultural
alienation and cultural reclamation, loneliness and human
kinship, memory, forgetting and loss.

Her first book, *'Others' Is Not A Race*, won the Singapore
Literature Prize 2018 (Creative Nonfiction).

Praise for *'Others' Is Not A Race*

'The thought-provoking collection of short stories
and essays reflects on being a Eurasian in Singapore,
explores the Eurasian identity and culture,
and questions the concept of race as a social construct.'
Her World, Singapore

'A most Singaporean book, from its grapples with life's
purpose and meaning to its scrummy paeans to local food
… It is the coming together of these micro-biographies
that eventually shape what we call collective
national histories too.'
Judges of the Singapore Literature Prize 2018

'Others'
Is Not A Race

Melissa De Silva

monsoon

monsoonbooks

Published in 2023
by Monsoon Books Ltd
www.monsoonbooks.co.uk

No.1 The Lodge, Burrough Court,
Burrough on the Hill, Melton Mowbray LE14 2QS, UK

ISBN (paperback): 9781915310224
ISBN (ebook): 9781915310231

First published in 2017 by Math Paper Press, Singapore.

A Cataloguing-in-Publication data record is available from the British
Library.

for Nanny

Contents

Introduction

A Eurasian is someone with both Asian and European ancestry. Many Singaporean Eurasians trace their heritage to European colonisation in Asia, first of the Portuguese back in the 1500s (in Malacca, Sri Lanka, Goa and Timor), then the Dutch (Malacca, Sri Lanka and Indonesia) and finally the British.

Each successive wave of colonial powers resulted in Eurasian children, from unions of the Europeans with Asian women. Bonded by the common religion of Christianity, (generally Catholicism) and the shared language of English, the Portuguese-Eurasians, Dutch-Eurasians and British-Eurasians in the Malayan region found it natural to intermarry.

Other Europeans like the Germans, French, Spanish and Italians arrived in Singapore during the colonial era as traders, part of shipping contingents or to set up businesses. Those who coupled with Asian women had children who were Eurasian too.

Over time, these diverse Eurasians drew together to form their own distinctive community. Their common experience of having both European and Asian ancestry, their unique position of straddling two cultures while ostensibly belonging to neither, was an important factor prompting them to come together as a cohesive group, one that was neither Asian nor European. In 1883 for instance, a group of Eurasians formed the Singapore Recreation Club, exclusively for Eurasians. This was the Eurasian community's response to the existence of European-only clubs such as the Singapore Cricket Club, formed in 1852, which at the time, barred entry to Asians and Eurasians.

According to the 2010 census, Eurasians comprised 0.4 per cent of the Singaporean population, or 15,581 people in total classified themselves as Eurasians. Unlike the Indians, Malays and Chinese, which have their own category under Singapore's multicultural policy (known as CMIO, which stands for 'Chinese, Malays, Indians and Others'), Eurasians are classified under the category 'Others'. This category used to refer predominantly to the Eurasians. In recent times however, the 'Others' category has expanded to include new citizens who do not fit into the categories of Indian, Malay or Chinese, such as Filipinos, Caucasians, Africans and Japanese. As such, Eurasians now find themselves in the same group as citizens who are not perceived as Singaporean from birth. This situation has bred further issues of identity for the Eurasian community, especially how they are perceived by other Singaporeans.

The Gift

They say that my language, like my grandmother, is dying.

'Hic!'

I am sitting next to Nanna on the polyester-covered sofa in her flat. On my forehead is a piece of paper the size of a postage stamp. It's been slapped on with spittle. My grandmother believes this will make the hiccups go away.

My cheeks are clammy. These inexplicable paroxysms are terrifying in my four-year-old world. Nanna takes my wrist in one hand. With her other hand, she makes a little man of two knobby-knuckled fingers and he begins walking up my arm as she chants the rhyme:

Gatu bai, gatu beng …

Her voice is playful and smiling. There is sun in it.

Buskah ratu …

The little finger man passes the crook of my inner elbow then clambers on to where my arm sprouts from my torso.

Naki teng!

As he jumps to his final destination, a flurry of tickling begins. I squeal and squeal.

Nanna laughs and draws me to her in an enveloping hug. She smells of olive oil – it makes her hair shine – and Lux soap and talcum powder. She smacks an exaggerated kiss on the top of my helmet of bowl-cut hair. She doesn't let on that my hiccups are gone.

'It's already a quarter past four. What you want for tea – butter cake?'

I shake my head so that my hair flaps in my face. Then I grin.

'Ah, I know … you waaant … chocolate rice toast! Right?' Nanna tweaks my nose and I yelp.

'Ya!'

Thickly buttered slices of pillowy white bread from the neighbourhood bakery, lavishly sprinkled with chocolate rice – a confection otherwise reserved only for baking cookies – is a treat my parents, away at work, never allow. I especially love tracing my finger in the glossy pools of melted butter and chocolate to make spirals and squiggles.

Nanna wipes a dribble of melted butter from my chin. 'So messy, the way you eat,' she tuts, but her eyes shine at me. They are strange eyes. Their lower lids slant upward in a severe sweep; that might have given her a cold, supercilious look, but instead, because of the playful expression on her mouth, they look mischievous, impish.

As I swing my legs and chomp into buttery-chocolate deliciousness, she ruffles my hair. I smile up at her, my cheeks full, my mouth still dribbly, secure in the knowledge of our shared secret.

* * *

In her eyes now, three decades later, there is no gleam of conspiratorial joy.

'Nanna, I love you,' I whisper.

I can't think of anything else to say. Nanna makes no response. She can't. There is a tube snaking into her strong, straight-bridged nose, delivering liquid nutrients from a can directly to her stomach three times a day. Her stroke six months earlier left the muscles around her mouth and throat semi-paralysed.

In the region of my upper left chest, I locate the now-familiar dull ache. I clasp her spindly hand and marvel that her face has weathered eighty-six years but hardly shows the signs. Where is the crêpey lattice cob webbing the elderly neck? The skin at her throat looks merely like well-handled paper, soft and pliable with use. As I kiss the top of her head, I inhale the scent of Johnson's baby powder.

What can I do for her? The same question, nagging me

for six months, circles back. It would be glorious if she could smile. If she had a reason to.

But I've never been a prattler. And my usual sardonic observations of life are hardly what she needs to lift her spirits as she confronts the tunnel's mouth of her mortality.

The words escape almost before I can think them solid.

Nanna j-jah kumi?

Have you eaten? A ridiculous question, given the food tube delivery system, but the question – a traditional Southeast Asian politeness – bubbles up; I'm speaking Kristang, on instinct.

I feel idiotic hearing the words tumble from me like bandy-legged children. Where is the rhythmic lilt I vaguely recall from her conversations with her sisters – now all gone – over thirty years ago, when I was the quiet grandchild sitting beside her at cherki jepun?

To me, Kristang was a sepia-tinted relic from the past. But to my grandmother, the language was alive and beating. It was the bond with her Eurasian mother and nine siblings, growing up in a black and white bungalow perched on MacRitchie Hill. It was the deliciously whispered language behind closed doors, out of fear of being heard by their Goan-Portuguese father. The stern, luxuriously moustachioed man banned Kristang at home. His children would master English, the tongue of the British and the route to power and security in Singapore in the 1920s.

So my grandmother's Kristang had been the language of childhood laughter and joking repartee, the heart's tongue of family intimacy. It was the linguistic mould that had shaped and cradled her thoughts.

Nanna doesn't seem to think I sound idiotic. Or perhaps she does. The right corner of her mouth twitches for a fraction of a second. I can't interpret exactly what that means. The ceiling fan blades try to keep the indolent 3pm heat at bay.

Heat fans up my throat and cheeks as I glance out the bedroom door. The chatter of my uncles and aunts floats toward me. One of them is regaling the others with tales of her seventeen-year-old.

'And so I told them, yes, of course my daughter can drive. She drives me round the bend!'

Peals of laughter.

Desperate that no one should burst into the room, I lean close to Nanna's ear and breathe:

Yo – jah kumi. Yo kumi … a-rus.

I stand there, feeling a disproportionate sense of achievement, having strung together this meagre utterance. I have just told her that I've eaten. I have eaten rice. With those two sentences, I'd exhausted my entire store of

Kristang vocabulary. It feels like I've just knelt to present my grandmother with a gift of … a rubber band.

The whirr of the fan is the only sound softening the silence. A few still seconds pass. Then Nanna squeezes my hand. Could it possibly be? Does she want me to continue? Then, as a pebble ripples the glassy film of a pool, I realise what I can do for her.

The next day, when I return with some material, a nervous energy runs from my neck to the soles of my feet. I feel like a stand-up comic about to debut in the spotlight.

'Nanna, remember you used to play this game with us?'

Gatu bai, gatu beng,
buskah ratu,
naki teng!

My grandmother's sparsely lashed eyes – once lustrously fringed – shutter slowly, deliberately, as if assuring me that yes, she remembers.

A flash of who and all she is overcomes me.

'Nanna, I'm going to get something from the kitchen. I'll come back soon, okay?' I pelt out of the room. I prop my elbows on the ledge of the kitchen window and stare out, unseeing, at lollipoped frangipani trees and people walking dogs. I cram clenched fists against my mouth and am glad for the pain of fingernails digging into my flesh. I exhale deeply and blot my cheeks with a crumpled tissue from my jeans' pocket.

I've always considered myself weak. Lacking the stoicism that one admires in people in novels or war stories who do heroic things with supreme calm. As I stand there, it occurs to me that this is the most difficult thing I have yet to do.

But as I walk back to the room, dry-cheeked, my head back, I seem less pathetic to myself, almost strong.

'Nanna,' I say, forcing sun into my voice, 'remember the story you used to tell us about the boy with the apples and the Saint Theresa statue?'

That night, in my own flat, I kneel by the rattan box in the corner of the storeroom. A veil of dust covers the pile of books within. I toss aside novels half-read then abandoned. Discarded romances surface, as well as hard covers on car engines. I fling them aside, raising mushroom clouds of dust. My nose and eyes are itching. As I sit back on my heels and sniffle, I spot it. Buried under a floppy handbook on flash photography. The *Kristang Dictionary*. I lift it out.

It had been a gift from an aunt years ago. As I open the large paperback tome, the pages are surprisingly unmottled. It was written by two school teachers setting down a legacy until then only ever passed down orally. I turn to a page at random:

A BRIEF INTRODUCTION TO KRISTANG –
A PEOPLE AND THEIR LANGUAGE

Alfonso d'Alburquerque, the hawkish, hook-nosed naval general who commanded the Portuguese fleet in 1511, soon found that Malacca was teeming with other peoples – Chinese, Arabs, Indonesians, Indians – also keen to profit from the lucrative spice trade between Southeast Asia and Europe. He promptly summoned reinforcements from home. The King of Portugal, instead of sending more warships, dispatched ordinary Portuguese men and women to populate the town, choosing the path of peaceful, though insidious propagation and assimilation within the local community.

*The new Portuguese immigrants married the local Chinese, Malays and Indians. The Portuguese tongue, planted in rich Malaccan soil, took into itself the complex wealth of its environment, absorbing words from the Straits Chinese (*chap chye *– a mixed vegetable dish), the Malays (*brani *– brave, daring;* chinchaloh *– fermented shrimp relish) and the Indonesians (*jimat *– a careful spender), to blossom into an exotic Malayanised European linguistic rose, unique in all of Asia and Europe.*

I flip to the dictionary section proper and find myself at K – *kara* – face, *kara feu* – ugly. Suddenly I'm back at one of my grandmother's cherki afternoons where I sit unheard, unseen. The resident gossip is gabbling about how pretty her grandson's new fiancée is. A grand aunt with tightly scraped back hair bends her head toward my grandmother and mutters, '*Kara feu!*' The frickative 'f' bears the full force of her scorn. Nanna flaps open her cotton and lace fan and covers her mouth.

There is more.

Grammatical Structure; Music and Song; Festivals and Cuisine. For the predominantly Catholic Portuguese-Eurasians, festive occasions are the major events on the religious calendar, times for boisterous family gatherings centred around food.

Indeed. Two weeks before Christmas, Nanna would be rolling out shortcrust pastry on the dining room table using the same wooden rolling pin she'd been using since she married at eighteen. The pastry would form the shell of pineapple jam tarts. She'd press out the scallop-edged discs with a brass and wooden mould. In a monster of a cauldron was pineapple jam. Fifteen hand-grated pineapples had been slow-cooked over a gentle fire every day for a week, inviting the alchemy of pulpy yellow froth into a sticky mass of burnished gold. The air would be a syrupy mist of cinnamon and clove-perfumed vapours that clung to our hair and clothes.

Already prepared a month before and standing sentinel on the kitchen shelves were rows of achar jars. A fiery medley of green mango preserves – dried in the sun, salted, vinegared and spiced – and the milder vegetable pickle of cucumber, carrot and cauliflower. And on the highest shelves sat the brandy-drenched fruitcakes and plum puddings made in October, maturing with dignified grace.

The following week, the smells of baking pastry and caramelised pineapple would be replaced with the almond-vanilla wafts of sugee cake.

'You really want to put that in the oven?' Nanna would say, questioning the results of letting me entertain myself with bits of dough.

The pale-yellow dough of the pineapple tart I'd been working on all afternoon had taken on a dubious grey tinge. The mountain of pineapple jam I'd fashioned in the pastry case was three times the height of Nanna's smooth pastry domes. And, I'd also tried to sculpt a pair of mouse ears from pastry at the very peak.

I nodded. Nanna frowned and put it in the oven anyway. Somehow though, I'd could never find my creations in the vast terrain of pastries left to cool on parchment later.

There is a recipe for pineapple tarts and sugee cake in the dictionary. There are nursery rhymes, like *Gatu Bai, Gatu*

Beng, and prayers. I clasp the book to my chest. I sit back on my heels, and feel sparklers going off inside me, very slowly.

I'm sitting down to my breakfast of muesli the next morning, running through the freshly memorised words now in my head, *tar di nanas*, *farinya*, *asah kukis*, when the phone rings.

It is my aunt, her voice wet.

'Your Nanna ...'

The receiver tumbles from my hand, its spiral cord snaking over the edge of the table, dangling just above the floor, winding and unwinding in a silently creaking pirouette.

'Hello? Girl? You there?'

The scores of words and phrases will be now left ungifted. I'd imagined presenting them in careful rations, one or two each day, to stretch out the joy over the next few months. At the very least, a few months. Now, they would remain unspoken, unheard, gifts without a receiver, floating between this world and the next, belonging nowhere.

* * *

Two months later, I'm about to sit down to dinner at the kitchen table in my flat. Beside the plate of rocket and rice curry salad, taped to the table is a piece of white card with the word *basiu* scrawled on it in black marker. Another piece of card is taped to the table next to the glass of water and says *glas* (*agu*). My spoon and fork have labels sellotaped to them so the ink won't run when they're washed. They're *kuleh* and *garfu* respectively. All over my kitchen and throughout my tiny apartment, white labels are plastered on appliances, flowerpots, chairs, shelves.

The one on the wooden model of a Portuguese warship on the coffee table in the living room says *caravel*. The vessel faces the South China Sea. My hours of research these past months tell me that this was the direction our seafaring ancestors came from to set up a trading base in Malacca.

At the height of its use in the seventeenth century, not only was Kristang adopted by the Dutch colonials who came after the Portuguese, but every Malaccan spoke it, from the Hokkien merchants bargaining for fish from Portuguese trawlers to the Tamil and Cantonese children playing hopscotch with their friends in the suburbs.

I found it astounding that our language had been spoken by all those people in all their variety, so long ago.

I had also been experimenting. Mention the word 'Kristang' in Singapore today, and you draw blank stares. Even its name sounds as obscure as geographical points in ancient Roman Iberia: Lucentum, Azalia, Kristang …

Today, in Malaysia and Singapore, it's one of Southeast Asia's vanishing linguistic jewels; only roughly five thousand people speak it. And we'd never thought to record it. Perhaps we'd assumed it would always be with us. But the knot of surviving speakers grows smaller every year as white heads droop and wrinkled lids close for the last time. And with them a lifetime of customs and laughter, repartee and colour, leach into the dust of unmemory.

Their middle-aged children know only a smattering of phrases. They'd embraced English during the 1950s and 1960s; the lingua of American and British pop culture. It had cachet. It was the language of Elvis, The Beatles and Bob Dylan. And they would later tell their own children who asked that English was the mother tongue of Eurasians. So in an absent reply over the evening news or a television game show, five centuries of cultural legacy was shrugged off into oblivion.

But today, I have found some strength from it.

I run my eyes, with their strangely upward slanting lower lids, over the snowfall of labels in my apartment. I will gather to myself these lost words of my ancestral tongue and I will speak them to my children and my children's children. This gift I can give them. The gift of knowing and being who they are, and who and all they have been.

And we will form a single, unbroken thread, stretching from my youngest grandchild, winding backward to the admiral, apothecary or merchant at the root of our heritage, perhaps five hundred, a thousand or even more years ago in that maritime European nation across many seas. And our language will course through the line, life-giving blood, linking us in a circlet of our common love of laughter and the simple joys of existence. We are, all of us and Nanna, inextricably bound unto eternity.

I lift a forkful of salad leaves and rice to my mouth. '*Basiu, garfu, agu* ...' I recite to myself as I begin chewing.

Let Them Eat (Sugee) Cake

I am having tea with my friends Annie and Grace at a glass box café perched on the edge of a park. The menu proudly asserts that something they served us was 'Brandy Sugee Cake'. But there's no getting around it, the cake sucks. Fine, maybe 'sucks' is too harsh, but one mouthful revealed the pretty triple-layered cake was simply cosmetic. It wasn't what a sugee cake was meant to be; what it could be.

Now, sugee is a dense cake, made from semolina flour, known as sugee in some parts of the Indian subcontinent. Sugee is the high-gluten endosperm portion of the wheat grain, used to make the brandy-impregnated cake traditionally served at Eurasian weddings, enrobed in marzipan and royal icing. It is a hefty cake that isn't shy about its weight, not like those whipped mousse and crème fraiche constructions that could blow away on a puff of cloud.

When you cut into this yellow cake, the scent of the ground almonds is released, combined with the aroma of brandy. Royal icing. That too wasn't named for being shy and retiring. It's an icing that holds its head high, completely unabashed about being a high-glycemic roller coaster of ninety percent icing sugar, with afterthoughts of egg whites and lemon juice. And marzipan, made from ground almonds, powdered sugar and egg whites, has to be rolled out in a thick slab, almost wrestled with, so much does it have a will and mind of its own. These two are destined to pair with the grainy nuttiness of sugee.

My friend Annie tastes it. Her mouth goes into a funny line. Then she tastes the slice of carrot cake with cream cheese icing.

'This cake is better than that one,' she says, meaning the carrot cake.

'They're just two different cakes,' I say.

I know I sound feeble. I want to speak up for sugee, to defend it, but I feel my words will lack conviction in the face of this forlorn example. The insipid butter cream is all wrong. It doesn't have the necessary heft, in grammage and flavour, to carry the sugee. I was looking forward to a giggly catch up with my two former colleagues from my magazine staffer days. I didn't come prepared for an off-the-cuff defence of a foundation stone of my edible heritage.

Eventually, after more clinking of forks against china in silence, I abruptly say, 'It's the wrong type of icing.'

My friends have no response to this. Indeed, I wouldn't blame them for thinking I'm off my rocker. Barely after the words are out of my mouth, I feel the sinking sense of discouragement of a person babbling in a foreign marketplace. My dear friends do not know the glories of Eurasian sugee. How could I show them the splendour of this confection?

Grace prods at at the mean spread of butter cream in between the top two layers of cake with her fork. 'Where's the brandy?'

'The brandy is supposed to be in the cake batter, but I don't think there's much of it,' I say. My heart refuses to commit to this defence. I am unsure of my allegiance to this particular representative of the sugee species. Did this jacked-up three-layered blimp have anything to do with me? Was it my kin? Or was it a mere hipster pretendster? Something whole and pure stripped of everything that had given it meaning, to be regurgitated as yet another curated dish/bicycle/herb pot by urbanites made homogenous by their cosmopolitan connectedness and uniform consumption of the same blockbuster TV series, 'lifestyle experiences' and new-made-old tchotchkes?

I don't think so.

'I didn't taste any brandy,' chimes Annie.

The brandy added into the batter would evaporate during baking so only a perfume of curranty mellowness remained. This thing here smelled blandly vanilla. I retreat into moody silence.

Hours later at my desk at home, as I sit in front of my laptop and procrastinate about starting work, I ask myself why I said nothing. Nothing about why, to match the density of the sugee cake, one needed an equally characterful, dense icing. Why, for our weddings, Eurasians serve sugee cake enfolded in marzipan and royal icing (there was fruit cake too, but that seems out of fashion). Is my throat chakra blocked or something? I wish I had that excuse. I am totally clueless how sugee has come to be the ultimate Eurasian wedding cake. Lacking this basic information, embarking on any type of explanation/awareness-raising campaign would open an embarrassing Pandora's box of ignorance.

Some nights later, I send my two friends a text:

ANNOUNCEMENT: I'm going to make a traditional 'this is how we do it at Eurasian weddings' sugee cake and I'm inviting you, at either of your places, to eat this project!

Annie texts back to offer her home and says she has beer and wine. I refrain from being anal and saying that beer and wine would kill the flavour of the cake. Instead, I think about dessert wine, like a beautiful syrupy moscato.

I go to my book case and leaf through the brown paper *Ricette di Cucina* I got when I was studying Italian in Tuscany years ago, and had taken half a year off from my magazine job.

There were recipes written in the hand of my Swedish

housemate for a parmesan eggplant bake, my German housemate for her grandmother's cake and photocopied cutouts of American sweets like brownies. My memory turns out to be correct. In my own hand is the recipe for sugee cake, my mother's secret recipe, which she refuses to give out except to a privileged inner circle (which basically comprises my sister and me).

On the day of the tea, I wake up at 6.30am. I need to leave for an appointment at 8.45 that morning, so I figure that would give me an hour to prep and an hour for the cake to bake, with time to spare. I'd set out and measured the ingredients the night before. I'd also beaten the sugee and butter together in the electric mixer until they became white and creamy, and left that to sit overnight. The idea is to let the sugee grains absorb the butter, for a softer cake. The sugee-butter mixture was on the kitchen table under a floral-patterned food cover. They would be folded into the batter later.

Right now, I needed to separate eggs. Four yolks to go into the sugar in one bowl. In another bowl, four whites for beating into the meringue. The flour and ground almonds were pre-measured in another two bowls. Being so together with bowl organisation does wonders for your self-esteem, I'm finding. Now I'm starting to see why some of those cooking show hosts who rustle up dishes from twenty-five bowls of prepped ingredients strut around like demigods.

After the yolks and sugar have been creamed in the mixer, I begin folding the flour into the egg yolk-sugar mixture. Then the chopped almonds, brandy and vanilla. Soon it becomes a fluffy batter, flecked with sugar granules. As I'm conscientiously folding away, the oven light goes. It's ready.

The last step is to fold in the whipped egg whites. I give the handwritten recipe in my mum's clear plastic folder a quick scan. Yup, we are good to go.

Even though it's the end of January, I've buttered the inside of a red and white Christmas cake tin. It has reindeer and snowflakes on it. If you don't look back, Christmas is a long way away. But why not enjoy a little bit of Christmas every day, I think gleefully as I pour in the batter, like some unseasonably festive elf.

The tin slides in, the oven door clangs shut. The snowflake tin rests inside, yellow batter glistening under the oven's tungsten light. As I look at the clock on the tiled kitchen wall, I feel a thrill. I am super organised and on time and I've baked a cake before breakfast. I rock.

After washing up, I'm about to step out of the kitchen.

Then my eye lands on the food cover on the kitchen table. 'Oh my lord, the sugee!'

The cake is happily baking without the sugee and butter mixture I'd left out overnight.

I grab the mitts, yank open the oven door and pull out the tin. When I hold my palm over the surface of the batter, there are no ripples of warmth. Miraculously, the sides of the tin are cool as well. The cake doesn't seem to have started baking.

Feeling decidedly undemigod-like, I fold the sugee-butter mixture into the cake batter. This is so stupid it's hilarious. I shove the thing in the oven again and hope I don't have to resort to bringing crackers for tea instead.

An hour later, all the pain and mayhem are forgotten. A light, golden-crusted cake sits on the kitchen counter. It's even risen a half inch over the top of the tin, like a soufflé. This must be what new mothers feel like. Pride, I mean, not soufflé.

While I'm snapping a photo, a thought occurs to me. Did I actually say 'Oh my lord, the sugee' just now? I have never, in my entire life, uttered that phrase. What am I, someone's aunt from the Deep South? I crop the photo and send it to my friends with an appropriately Christmassy caption, still feeling weirded out by my Southernism. Then, finally, I get it.

I've officially become ... a Eurasian Sugee Auntie.

Later that afternoon, in Annie's kitchen, I also realise I am becoming scarily possessive about the cake. It sits resplendent on the granite island counter, its cardboard box lid open. Annie's two chihuahuas, Barley and Toto, are looking up, hopeful.

'I'll cut it,' says Annie, reaching for a knife.

'No, *I'll* cut it,' I say.

Annie looks like she has doubts about my sanity. I have doubts about my sanity too. Knife tussle moment over, I focus on trying to slice the cake like a normal person and not have my friends disown me before the tea event has even begun.

When I carry the three plates into the living room, I get a flash of what Masterchef contestants must feel like bringing their food up to the judges' table. There is the excruciatingly slow cutting of cake with fork, the slo-mo journey of a million miles of fork to mouth, jaws clamping shut frame by frame, the chewing, the chewing that stretches unto eternity.

'Mmmm, this is so good!' says Annie. Grace makes a sort of squeak.

Oh my god, what?

Her face lights up the way it does when she has a devious plan. 'Mel! Do you think I can order this from you for my relatives for Chinese New Year?'

Sugee Cake: A (Very Brief) Speculative History

While many Eurasians know how to make (and eat) sugee cake, ask them how it came to be part of our cuisine and you will likely get a sheepish shrug. The origins of this cake – made of semolina, wheat flour, ground almonds, eggs, butter and sugar, fragrant with brandy – remain mysterious, strange given that it is synonymous with Eurasian celebrations, marking life's major milestones. A Eurasian baby entering the world will often find itself sharing the spotlight with a beautifully iced sugee cake at its Baptism party. Sugee cake often presides over the wedding of a Eurasian couple, where it looks down on the bride and groom in the form of a tiered affair encased in marzipan and royal or fondant icing. No Christmas is complete without sugee cake on the table. Often there are silent competitions between aunties who seem to be innocently chewing cake at a host's home, all the while making shrewd assessments about whose cake is lightest. A sad day indeed for the baker whose sugee cake is judged by guests as 'rough'. Even sadder is the dreaded pronouncement: 'heavy like stone'. And finally when it's time to depart this earth, sugee cake is often served at a Eurasian funeral.

One clue to its origins might be its main ingredient and namesake. Sugee, or semolina, is durum wheat that is more coarsely ground than regular wheat flour. Semolina is what good pasta is made of, as well as gnocchi. Sugee is widely used in India, in savoury dishes like idli and the dessert halwa. In South India, it is known as rawa, and is used to make rawa dhosai. In Singapore, many of us would recognise it in the form of the sugee biscuits that used to be sold at mamak shops.

Could sugee cake have originated in India, as a cross-cultural hybrid resulting from European colonialism? Cakes and pastries are foreign imports to India. There is generally no baking done in ovens in Indian cuisine. The only exception is in the cylindrical clay oven called the tandoor, introduced to South Asia from the Middle East. But European-style pastries and cakes cannot be successfully baked in this sort of oven. Traditional Indian desserts are all made on the stovetop. They may be steamed, toasted, boiled in syrup, deep-fried. The North Indian dessert kheer is a thick rice pudding cooked on the stove, studded with nuts and raisins. Fritters like jalebis, the twisted dough strands soaked in syrup, are deep-fried. Laddus, found all over India, are made of chickpea batter, dripped into hot fat to form crisp little dough drops. These are then drenched in sugar syrup and shaped into balls. Stovetop desserts, all of them.

Goa is the only region in India which has a five-hundred-year-old tradition of baking. Is it a coincidence that Goa is a former Portuguese colony? One of the traditional Christmas cakes in Goa today is baath cake, also known as Goan coconut and semolina cake. Goan cooks of centuries past might well have incorporated a more affordable local ingredient, the grittier semolina flour, into a cake to save on more expensive refined wheat flour. This would still enable them to turn out an impressive 'foreign' baked confection. The dense cake might have been such a pleasing result that it travelled with the Portuguese and Indo-Portuguese to Malaya in the 1500s. Perhaps an enterprising woman there happened to have some ground almonds on hand, and decided to add them to the mixture for an extra rich Christmas cake? And brandy, synonymous with Christmas pudding, might have seemed a natural addition to the festive cake too. Or perhaps the addition of brandy was for more practical reasons, to help the cake's keeping qualities in the days before refrigerators? It may be impossible to ascertain for sure, but these are fun conjectures about how we got to the version that graces Eurasian life today.

Meeting with the Sea

I am nine.

I am in Primary Three, in social studies class at the all-girls Convent of the Holy Infant Jesus. Not all of us are Catholic (we even have some Muslims in the enrolment) and unlike in my mother's day when sweet Irish nuns taught classes, none of our teachers are nuns except one who makes me think of a bespectacled cockroach. That day, the social studies lesson promises pleasant disruption because we have to move out of the classroom to the air-conditioned video lab. We also get to choose our seats, and I choose to sit with my three friends (we're the only ones in class who study Malay as a second language): Faranaz Alam, Michelle Joseph and Geraldine Minjoot.

When the chatter and movement across the room finally settles, Ms Pat Lim, a short, chunky woman with a porky sort of face, casts her eye over us.

'Those four Indian girls sitting together, split up!'

My three friends and I look at one another. Who was she talking to? Faranaz is of Pakistani descent; Geraldine is Eurasian, like me. Only Michelle is Indian.

'I said move!' she snaps.

She clearly means us. We are alarmed. Being nine, and cowed by the authority of a teacher, we break apart and manage to find random seats among the rest of the pupils. I'm not able to articulate the sense of unfairness I feel, like a hot, clenched fist. But during the rest of the lesson, and as I sit brooding on the public bus that afternoon, I can't shake my conviction – what she'd done was wrong. Why shouldn't we have been allowed to sit together? Never mind that she was ignorant only one of us was Indian. Every single one of the rest of our class was Chinese – all thirty of them – and they were sitting all together, weren't they?

I am twenty-five.

I am trying to communicate with the immigration official at the airport in Barcelona. He is speaking in Spanish, and I respond in my newly acquired broken Italian, refusing to lapse into English, because I'm ridiculously determined not to stick out as even more of a tourist. He is stony-faced when he accepts my red Singaporean passport. Then he flips it open and his eyes glide over my surname. His expression lifts.

'De Silva,' he enunciates perfectly. 'You are Portuguese?'

'*Il mio nonno.*' My grandfather. Now, that's not exactly true. But I don't know how to say 'great-grandfather' in Italian so I can't tell him it was my great-grandfather who was from Goa and he was only part Portuguese. But none of this seems to matter.

'*Muy bueno!*' He beams genuine welcome at me and I experience a strange warm feeling I've never felt at Changi Airport returning home.

I am thirty-five.

I am in a cab on the way to the Eurasian Association at Ceylon Road. The taxi driver eyes me openly in the rear-view mirror.

'Miss, you are what *ah*?'

I've moved beyond my teenage belligerence, when I would either not acknowledge they were referring to my race or retort, 'Human.' I don't even roll my eyes anymore, even in my head. I think I've come a long way.

'Eurasian.'

'What is *loo*-rayshiun?'

'People who are mixed. Europe people and Asia people mixed together.'

'Aww ... like Gurmit Singh issit?' he says, referring to the Singaporean comedian.

'Er ... no. Uncle, Gurmit Singh is Chinese and Indian. His surname is "Singh", so – never mind.'

I've never understood why it seems so difficult to understand. No doubt we make up less than one percent of the population, but we've been part of this country since the colonial times, as long as some and longer than others.

We spend the rest of the journey in silence, zooming

past skeletons of condos rising from stamp-sized plots of land, regurgitated tarmac and clay from road works and the boarded-up Red House Bakery on East Coast Road, its shophouse face shuttered and mute. This is Singapore. Where you'd be a fool to cling to any place held dear, where the treasures of space and memory being blasted into oblivion is the only certainty in the ferocious race for development. The red brick National Library where my mother used to take me since I was two, demolished to make way for a yawning traffic tunnel. Block 28 Lorong 6 in the Toa Payoh neighbourhood, where I lived with my grandparents till I was five, razed to the ground. Thank god the dragon playground in front of the building was spared, out of a government nod at 'preservation' and 'Singapore icons'.

Some minutes later we approach the gates of our destination.

'Okay uncle, you can stop here please.'

As the taxi rolls to a halt, the driver cranes his neck to look at the massive three-storey building in the middle of the leafy residential neighbourhood. 'What is this place? Your house *ah*?'

'No, this is the Eurasian Association.'

'*Har*?'

'For Eurasian people, mixed people, mix European and Asian.'

Still not rolling my eyes.

'Oh, United Nations *ah?*'

In December that year, I make a trip to Malacca, Malaysia. The Portuguese Settlement is a coastal hamlet of modest, mostly single-storey houses spanning three lanes on either side of the impressively named d'Alberqueque Road. As I walk along the main road, an old man with sun-creased skin turns his head as he cycles by. A wavy-tressed teenaged girl and two boys chatting across a gate pause in their conversation, watching me silently as I pass. The stranger in the village. What's even weirder is I'm overcome with a feeling of kinship with these sun-browned, curly-haired people I've never seen before.

In the 1500s, when the Portuguese arrived at the palm and mangrove-fringed coastal town of Malacca, on the west coast of the Malay Peninsula, their imperative was to capture control of the lucrative maritime trade passageway between Asia and Europe. As time went on, the union of the Portuguese with the local women resulted in the burnished-skinned children with Iberian features, and a culture that leaned heavily toward the religion, customs and language of the male colonisers. Five hundred years later, this tiny Catholic community, with a robust Latin tendency towards music, dance and enjoying the sweetness of life, still endures in the midst of the Muslim-majority country. A month earlier, in November, I was in Uncle Maurice Pereira's living room in the Portuguese Settlement (formed in 1926 to help consolidate the Portuguese-Eurasian community). The rain was driving down against the slatted wooden shutters. His fisherman's hands, weather worn, were clasped on his lap. My father's cousin was bare-bodied, wearing only white loose cotton pyjama trousers, and his still-muscled torso made him look like a jujitsu master. He regarded me with eyes of blue traced around dark lenses, the onset of cataracts.

My great-grandfather had been a fisherman in Malacca, the traditional livelihood of this community descended from the seafaring Portuguese. My father had told me how, when he was a boy, he would accompany his mother – who moved to Singapore with his father after WWII to seek a better life – to Malacca during the school holidays. There, he'd learned from his grandfather how to make two foods from the fishermen's catch: chinchalok, the relish of shrimp fermented in salt and brandy; and belachan, heavily salted, fermented shrimp paste, baked into hard cakes in the sun, excellent stir fried with vegetables and a generous handful of chilli.

As I explained how I'd like to document his work by going out fishing with him, to record it for future generations, his craggy white eyebrows rose.

'You want to write something? About me?'

That Saturday morning in December, it's just past 8.30am when I set off with Uncle Maurice and his eighteen-year-old grandson, Jeremy, in his open boat named *Lucy*. His cropped close white bristles are hidden under a black cap and he's wearing a white polo tee that says 'Irish Harrier Pub' on the back.

The water glitters. My notebook and camera are waterproofed in plastic and ready to go. At my feet at the bottom of the boat is a one-day-use orange lifejacket, still in its clear wrap, and the fishing nets. The planks we sit on are worn smooth, bleached by the sun. Even if I run my fingers along the edge of the boards, I don't feel any splinters.

Soon we are speeding through the waves and Maurice is pointing out spots on the shoreline where, in the 1950s, they would push their boats through the mud of the mangroves at 5am, carrying their water for the day in glass bottles ('Those days no one had a fridge').

We approach a boat with a flapping orange and yellow flag, carrying two Eurasian fishermen, a father and paunchy son, and a Malay boatman. A white buoy attached to a stick with a red flag bobbing nearby indicates where their net is.

'They are fishing for pomfret,' says Maurice.

He asks them how it's going. There's no need to reply. As they draw up the net, it sparkles like fairy candyfloss, then we see they've only caught three tiny fish, smaller than a child's palm. The son tosses a plastic bag caught in the net back into the sea.

Maurice's voice takes on a hard edge. 'All the fish dying, all the construction, the reclamation.'

We are soon scudding past a small island, called Pulau Jawa, just off Malacca's coast. 'In the '60s, we would go camping there, to fish, eat sardines and gather seaweed to make jelly,' Maurice tells me, his sea otter face crinkled with glee.

Pulau Jawa was where the Portuguese naval general Alfonso d'Albuquerque first dropped anchor on July 1st, 1511, as he led a fleet of eighteen ships, with nine hundred Portuguese men and three hundred Goan-Indians, sailing in on his carrack, the *Flor de la Mar*.

Uncle Maurice points to undulations of pale grey mounds in the distance on the water. His forearms are compact and sleek with muscle, lined with protruding veins. 'See what happened,' his eyes rest on the coastline of developments, 'to our sea.'

Sand barges lie like alien spacecraft beside them and the air is filled with metallic hissing sounds. These piles of sand are the nascent artificial islands of Melaka Gateway, a project with ambitions to be the largest cluster of synthetic islands in Southeast Asia. The plan for the 246-hectare area is to hold entertainment resorts, theme parks and 'man-made eco-islands'. 'We fishermen don't cry ah? *Habis, habis lah*,' he says in Malay. When it's gone, it's gone.

As I look, I think of my great-grandfather, the fisherman, and imagine the times he'd shared with my own father, passing on traditions that had survived for over five centuries.

And now, three just generations later, the thread of all this knowledge and richness would be snapped. My retired father had been trained as a mechanic. As for myself, former women's magazine journalist and urban princess, I'm hardly the material of a maritime professional.

A half hour later, we are having engine trouble. Maurice fiddles with the outboard motor but it doesn't revive. Smiley Jeremy, with blindingly white, straight teeth and an undercut with attitude, picks up the oar and rows. Without the low roar of the engine, the peace is velvet. The only sounds are the lapping of the sea against the boat and the swish of waves against the sun-bleached wood of the oar.

As we make our way slowly back to shore, Jeremy tells me he works for a local film production house called Marco Polo and has just completed a job working on a film set in Mongolia, filmed in a studio in Johor Bahru. His job was to look after the animals on the set. There were three pigs, two goats, a puppy and a lamb. When two of the pigs got into a scuffle, a piece of one pig's ear flew off. Jeremy saved it.

'It's brown now,' he says, sounding like a proud father. 'Soon I think it will be black.'

'Does it smell?' I ask.

He nods, dazzling me with a smile. 'Yes.'

Finally we make it to a ramshackle dock and Maurice trades boats with another fisherman. On the second leg of the trip, as we pass mangroves near Kampung Batang Pasir, the trees closer to the water's edge toppled like fallen soldiers, Maurice tells me the mangroves used to be alive with wild boars, monkeys and birds. This is where the fishermen would catch *siput*, sea snails, then cook them with slices of unripe papaya, small prawns and *santan*, coconut milk.

Here, the ocean is a translucent mud tint, like watery tea stirred with milk, with a greenish-blue rim along the horizon. Flakes of sun dance on the water and I'm gripped by the urge to swim, to glide through the cool. I lean over the boat's edge and trail my fingers through the waves, letting the water release in a delicious crest.

'We're coming to the place for fishing,' announces Maurice some time later, when the mangroves have become specks in the distance. I rummage in my bag and unwrap my camera from its plastic covering.

'Boy, where are the nets?' he asks Jeremy.

Jeremy stares at the floor of the boat as if encountering virgin terrain. He has the look of a boy who has misplaced the nets. There are the lifejacket, rope and a plastic container with money, sunglasses, a penknife and Maurice's mobile phone in it. They'd forgotten to load the nets when we swapped boats.

'If we go back one hour to get the net and come back, it will be too late for fishing already,' Maurice explains.

My heart flops. There was only today. Tomorrow he'd be off to the hospital to prepare for an eye operation for his cataracts, and he didn't know if and when he'd be fishing again.

I manage to nod. Maurice has been kind, hospitable and his company an absolute delight. I don't want him to feel bad. 'Never mind, Uncle. It's okay. I got to see the sea. We can go back.'

He cuts the engine. 'No hurry. We drift for a while. We relax.'

It was a clear distinction of values: manic urban efficiency vs. sea village chill. I feel slightly chastened, not by him but by my own embryonic Latin spirit. 'C'mon,' it prods me. 'Can't you even relax a little and enjoy being out at sea?'

I don't yet know what my Latin spirit looks like. I picture it maybe doing the flamenco, holding maracas, even though this is a culturally muddy, geographically inaccurate rendition. Is it a woman? Well, it looks olive-skinned, and seems to be wearing a red dress. But this just might be the subconscious influence of the WhatsApp emoticon of a woman in a red dress holding maracas I sometimes use.

Maurice points out a boat with a roof. He tells me how before, when they did night fishing, they would sleep in a boat like that. 'No mosquitoes!' He slaps his knee as if in triumph. 'If you get hungry, cook Maggie Mee, drink coffee. So nice!' His eyes shine. The man has a lifetime of happiness bottled inside him, I think, enough to last the rest of his time on earth. As my mind flashes to my previous career of chronically overstressed cubicle rat and the illness that finally produced, perhaps it's naïve romanticising, but I feel a deep tug of yearning for this hard yet idyllic life, and an ache for everything that's passed and will be lost forever.

Later, as the boat chugs slowly back to shore, I think about how I'd travelled all the way here to document one of the last Portuguese-Eurasian fishermen in Malacca, and our traditional livelihood. It seems almost funny it didn't happen. Almost. Maurice stirs me from my reverie with a gesture. He jerks his chin toward Jeremy, sitting at the bow. The massive construction for a hotel by the settlement's jetty forms a backdrop for his grandson's figure.

Maurice's tone is a wash of sadness over weary anger. 'Jeremy cannot be in this line already,' he says, meaning fishing. 'The sea is dead.'

His last words are muffled as the dull drone of a generator fills the air.

The next morning, on Sunday, I walk to the settlement's Chapel of the Immaculate Conception for Mass at 7.30am. The place is not jam packed like I expected but about seventy-five percent full. After I'm seated, I see the pew I've chosen has no kneeler. The polished ceramic tile floor looks practically spotless, far cleaner than the church floors in Singapore, where you can often spot stray hairs or dust bunnies. I decide to stay. Five minutes later though, the sun inching across the grid rectangle of window facing the pew is blinding.

I move to the adjacent pew. A dusky man with steel-rimmed spectacles is seated at the end, his head bent. I tap him on the shoulder and he makes way for me. Two minutes before the Mass starts, a short man with honeyed highlights smiles his way into our pew and takes a seat on my right. In Singapore, I can go weeks without seeing any other Eurasian except my own family. Here, I'm sandwiched between two Eurasian men, neither of whom are my relatives. This unprecedented scenario practically qualifies as being on a reality dating show.

During the Mass, the children are not heard, unlike the constant fidgeting, murmuring and some outright conversations between parents and their kids during services in Singapore. At one point, while we are standing, the boy of about six in the pew in front of me wiggles from his grandmother's grasp and scampers to sit and hug her from behind, burying his head in the small of her back. She takes his wrist and guides him gently to stand beside her. At no point during the Mass did I see anyone look at their mobile phones. This I like. This I like very much.

At intervals during the service, my eyes drift to the window. The early morning light bathes the brick wall beyond in a gold glaze and casts the wrought iron lamp outside into silhouette. The lamp looks like those I've seen in photos of Lisbon's streets. I've always wanted to visit Portugal, to see the place of my ancient ancestors, but now, perhaps there's no need. I realise why I feel so strangely comfortable in Malacca. I've found a place I can claim as my own.

After Mass I take a two-minute walk down to the beach. The sun is watery on the blue and open boats with peeling paint bob against the charcoal rocks. In the distance is a kelong structure, picturesque, made of long sticks. Three mudskippers the length of my index finger hop among the ropes mooring the boats.

As I move closer to the jetty, the air is filled with the metallic whine of drills and the clang of machinery. Relentless construction, even on a Sunday. Instead of the unfettered expanse of ocean, now the view from the settlement is blighted by the concrete monstrosity of the upcoming hotel a few hundred metres away, grasping for the sky. In the sea beyond are islands of powdery grey sand. In an alternate universe, they could be beautiful, like the humpbacked mounds of Vietnam's Halong Bay, if you ignore the fact that these are the offshoots of reclamation.

I remember how it felt to be out in the boat yesterday, the lapping of the waves, the caress of the breeze, the sear of heat on skin. When I started out for Malacca just two days ago to document a vital piece of my heritage, I didn't imagine I'd be setting off on a journey to the place where I'd finally feel like I belong. Yet this place too, is having its identity eroded by the relentless claw of development. Is it selfish of me that my joy still outweighs my sadness? What I do know is that this is the only patch in the world where I don't have to explain who I am, or why. There is such relief at being able to walk among people like me, unexplained and understood. The feeling is euphoric.

Tok, tok, tok. The sound of hammering infuses the morning. The sun's soft light filters through the green netting shrouding the concrete structure, as the yellow hard hats scurry about their business. I turn my back to it all and start making my way down the beach, the noise of industry growing fainter with each step.

Moulmein Rise
and Jalan Bahagia

AS TOLD TO MELISSA DE SILVA
BY HER MOTHER, GWENNE PINTO

When I was in primary three, this was in the 1950s, we went to MacRitchie Reservoir – my cousins Tony and John, together with my brothers Victor and Conrad. Conrad was the youngest at that time. He might have been in primary one. The two ringleaders were Tony and Victor, the two oldest. Uncle Victor is two years older than me. We told our parents we were going and I remember your Nanny making sandwiches and some ubi kayu Malay kueh for us to take along. It's tapioca, coloured pink and rolled in coconut. I think they grate the tapioca, then steam it, then roll it in coconut.

So we took the bus from our house in Moulmein Rise. First we walked along a roughly paved path along the edge of the reservoir, then it became a muddy track. Then we came to the water's edge. We had no choice but to cross the reservoir. I doubt it would have been across the whole reservoir, that would have been too big. But we reached a part where we couldn't walk any more so we had to cross from one bank to the other. There was a kind of metal pole, most likely a water pipe, across the water, so we had no choice but to sit on it and slowly slide ourselves across the pipe, one by one. Then it was Conrad's turn. He was so scared when he got to the middle, he refused to move any more! He just remained stuck there and started crying! So either Victor or Tony had to inch back along the pipe to help him get across.

When we got home it was later than our parents expected us. We got a scolding because first thing, we were late. And of course your Grandpa wanted to know what took us so long. They thought we were just going to go there, eat and come back. Of course, then Conrad started crying. Then the whole story came out. The same night, Conrad got sick, he had a fever and vomited. So we all got scolding lah. Nanny prepared the food because they thought we were just going to have a picnic on the grass, not hike around the whole place.

Moulmein Rise is on a bit of a slope. We lived along a row of houses. The walls of the houses were quite thin, you could hear when our neighbours shouted. Today's terrace houses are a luxury compared to those. You don't see those kinds of houses any more. Some parts were made of cement, some parts wooden boards.

The back of our Moulmein Rise house faced the Jewish

graveyard. I heard the boys daring each other, to go at night and sit in the graveyard. I can't recall if they ever did it. I doubt it, because Grandpa would have known if they had left the house at night. But I did hear them talking about it and I didn't want to have any part of it!

From the back of our house, you could walk past the Jewish cemetery and go down to Novena church. That was our Sunday Mass place.

At the bottom of the slope, there was a very big, empty bungalow house. It was on stilts, but not your flimsy wooden stilts. It was bricks. We used to go there and play because it was empty and there were the big grounds of the garden. There was a red jambu merah tree. My cousin Tony would use a stick and try and bring the fruit down. Then one day we discovered that in the area underneath the house – I don't know what made us go and explore it – there was a picture of a person, and there were some joss sticks. That scared us like mad, and we began saying 'Oh, it's a ghost!' So later we began calling it the 'Ghost House'. We would scare ourselves talking about it, yet we would purposely want to go there.

At Christmas, Nanny would make pineapple tarts. It was not like the small, dainty little things we have now. Oh yes, what we have now is considered dainty. Those tarts were the size of drinking glasses! She would roll out the dough and cut out circles with glasses. Then she would cut strips of dough and put it around the edge of each circle of dough to make a hollow to put in the jam. It was very laborious, not like now. When all the jam was in the pastry shells, she would take a sharp scissors and cut little strips of dough. We would make these into little patterns, like a V shape to put on the top of the jam. We would wash the tops of the tarts with egg glaze.

We had no oven then. Across the road from our house, there was a market and next to the market was a bakery. We used to bring the tarts down to the bakery and the guy would bake it for us, then we would come and collect it. Sometimes it would be burnt but we were so happy to eat the stuff, we didn't care if it was burnt or not! Every tart was very precious.

My cousins Tony, John and Girl (her real name is Rita but we used to call her Girl) also lived along the same row of houses, so we were all very close. We played together and at night, Grandpa would check all our homework. He would also teach us together. There was a Chinese family along the row that we were very friendly with. I think the boy's name was Richard. Other than my school friends, those were my 'home friends', so to speak. We didn't stay there very long. We moved to Jalan Bahagia after that.

We lived in another row of houses at Jalan Bahagia in the 1960s. There was a kind of cement porch running along the front doors of the houses there. So you could put seats outside. It was a very kampung-ish kind of thing. I remember auntie Margaret and auntie Emily, my mother's sisters, and my parents used to do sit there and talk in the evenings. We also used to wait at night for the hawkers to come. I just cannot remember what on earth the hawkers were selling!

The Indian bread man would come in the afternoon and we would go and buy bread. There was no such thing as butter. We would have margarine – candle wax-looking margarine, now that I think about it – and the kaya was some kind of orangey-brown globby thing, but we were very happy to be able to get that. That was heaven already.

Water rationing was common and I was thankful I had strong brothers – Victor, Conrad, Ivan and Jerry – to carry those buckets of water home. Our home in Jalan Bahagia became flooded at least once a year. My brothers helped Grandpa carry the furniture and fridge upstairs. Sometimes the waters came up too fast and the furniture would be ruined and have to be replaced. Jalan Bahagia was a lovely place to stay, because of the garden in the front and back. Your grandmother planted lots of herbs, like sirih and lengkuas. We even had a white rabbit in the garden. And we had made so many friends among our neighbours, it was like a kampung.

Yet the constant flooding caused my father, who was the most patient man I know, to say that he had had enough. When I was in CHIJ secondary, we moved to a two-room flat in Toa Payoh, all nine of us cramped in the flat.

Debal Encounters

Arnav is telling Diya about a lunch at Quentin's we attended a few months ago with some friends. 'It was a buffet of Eurasian food. It was fantastic!'

We are at the 24-hour Starbucks on the main shopping street in Singapore, Orchard Road. The crowd is braving humid tropical drizzle and rain-slick pavements, going about their errands with the determined ferocity that the last weekend before Christmas inspires. I nod absently. All I want to do is go to Hobbit Land. After all, I've been waiting a year. I am with two Indians, not Singaporeans of Indian descent, but true-blue spice-in-the-blood Indians from India. The wild-moustached Arnav, whose booming laugher will ricochet around a room and embrace you in its fold, and his friend Diya are from Bombay. They are in Singapore working for AXN and a public relations firm respectively. I would have preferred to go to a non-corporate-megalith café but such prime real estate, where upscale shops like Prada and Louis Vuitton jostle with the ubiquitous Zara and Uniqlo, does not encourage the independent retail spirit.

Anyway, this coffee is a mere 30-minute stopgap between us and the 3D High Frame Rate plunge that will land us in

Middle Earth for *The Hobbit: Battle of the Five Armies*.

This is the first time I'm meeting Diya. It turns out the married woman has a chummy relationship with Arnav, nurtured over cookout dinners among their clique of middle-class Indians from India living and working in Singapore. She sips her hazelnut latte and does not glance at me as she goes on about the various social gatherings they've attended together and the people they know in common.

That's fine. I'm happy to nurse my matcha soy latte and play the observer. Socially, I'm hardly the party performer. I find it thoroughly draining to have to spin yarns and constantly manage an audience like some master puppeteer. In smaller social settings, I'm also perfectly okay with sitting back and being the listener. This natural predilection may well have been enhanced by a decade of being a journalist, a professional of the art of active listening.

After Arnav's enthusiastic outburst, Diya picks at her muffin with her fork. 'What is Eurasian food?'

Dammit. Already, I sense danger on the horizon.

'Well, it's a mix of various influences, really. European, Chinese, Indian,' I say.

'Like what?'

I stare at the Adidas storefront across from us. 'Curries, stews, shepherd's pie ...' I trail off, awash in mortification. I realise I cannot call to mind a single name of a Eurasian dish in Kristang. And I'm telling a motherland Indian that curry is one of our native dishes. Why don't I just run around wearing a paper hat with 'Idiot!!' written on it? Maybe it's a low blood sugar thing. Maybe my brain just doesn't have the juice to extract details that have been shoved too far back in the mental filing cabinet.

Two weeks later, at a high tea gathering at a friend's place, the worst is confirmed. I am a culinary heritage cretin.

I am having a fine time catching up with friends, some of whom I haven't seen in almost a year. The uninterrupted stream of bubbly is also giving a pink-tinted glow to the occasion. My friend Nicole Batchelor, a gentle-natured human dove, whom I've only ever seen lose her temper while driving on holiday in Phuket, holds out her iPhone to me. It's an aerial shot of a white plate bearing three different hues of brown food.

'These are three traditional Eurasian dishes. Guess what they are?' she says, her eyes and face glowing.

I'm panicking here. More people are going to know I'm an utter fool. Then a brilliant idea strikes.

'Debal curry ...' I bluff, not even knowing which brown splotch it might be. But I'm sure I'll be right that debal is at least one of them, because it is the definitive classic Eurasian dish.

'Correct!' Nicole, whom I've known since we started school together at seven, doesn't seem to notice my cunning.

'And what about the other two?'

Crap. Come on brain, what are the other dishes? Try and remember a name, any name …

'Feng?' My querulous tone betrays me. Of course, I have no idea if and which of the two remaining brown fractions could be the spiced pork offal.

'And the other?' prompts Nicole encouragingly. I feel like a ridiculous four-year-old, trying to identify types of food illustrated on a cue card.

'Um …'

She looks expectant.

The tension is killing me. 'I don't know!'

'It's smoor.'

'Ah, right.'

Another dish of spiced pork.

I stare at the wheel of three browns. I feel like a huge disappointment. How could I be ignorant of decades, if not centuries, of culinary heritage? The answer is simple – I don't eat any of these foods.

Two years later, and I am in a very different place. I am now embarking for serious health reasons on a diet that is free of dairy, soy, refined sugar and meat. The question that faces me: how do I make food that isn't also free of taste? I think I have done pretty well these initial weeks, trying out new ingredients like nutty brown organic Italian lentils in my gluten-free ramen and using my new 1600w blender on 'bisque' mode to whiz up cannellini beans into a moussey thing with enough structure to stand up in peaks. Perhaps I'm a sucker for punishment, but I decide that the new blender is a great opportunity to try making debal again, which I haven't done in years. Even though I'm no longer eating meat, I decide to make it using chicken thighs and smoked ham bones. I'll just have a taste of the gravy, and feed the chicken to my carnivorous sister.

Debal curry is one of the more well-known Eurasian dishes, not least because many people think it's called 'Devil's curry'. This is a misnomer. 'Debal' is a Kristang word. What it means, I cannot say. I have asked some Kristang experts about this but haven't been able to glean anything other than, well, it's the name of a Portuguese-Eurasian curry.

Leaving the mystery of its etymology aside, what we do know is that originally, debal curry was made on Boxing Day. The dish was basically created to use up the leftover roasts and other meats from the Christmas feast of the previous day. That's why, if you've had the pleasure of sampling debal made by cooks from a range of families, it might seem a schizophrenic dish. The intrepid taster may discover any combination of the following: chicken, smoked ham bones, pork, turkey, beef, honey baked ham, even (as I can personally attest) char siew.

The Southeast Asian stamp on this curry is the lemongrass

and galangal. Other common ingredients in the rempah or spice paste are chillies, coriander, onions, mustard seeds, candlenuts and vinegar. Obviously my palate is biased, but like probably every other Eurasian, I think my mother's bright red debal is the best I've tasted. This is her recipe below, which she got from her aunt Emily Pinto, my maternal grandmother Patsy Pinto's older sister.

INGREDIENTS

10 dried chillis (or fewer if your heat tolerance is lower) 1 tbsp ground coriander

1 tsp mustard seeds

1-inch piece of fresh turmeric or 1 tsp turmeric powder 1 stalk of lemongrass

4 slices of galangal, about 1/4 cm thick each

3 cloves of garlic

1 piece ginger, about 1/2 inch

3 large onions

6 candlenuts

3 tbsp light soy sauce

2 tbsp white vinegar

1 chicken stock cube

1 kg chicken and smoked ham bones, pork or other meat

salt

2 tsp sugar, and more if needed
cooking oil

METHOD

Add dried chillies, coriander, mustard seeds, turmeric, lemongrass, galangal, garlic, ginger, onions and candlenuts to a blender. Add just enough water for the blender to be able to process the ingredients smoothly into a paste.

Heat oil in a saucepan. When oil is hot, fry the blended spice paste until aromatic. Add soy sauce, vinegar and stock cube. Add meat, then enough water to almost cover the meat. Season with salt and sugar. Cook until meat is tender when pierced with a fork. Taste and adjust seasoning again with more salt, sugar and/or vinegar if needed.

For me, this assertive, bright red curry has just the right amount of heat. Add the smokiness from the ham bones and the saliva-inducing acidity from the vinegar, and this combo of meat and gravy becomes something that dances on the tongue.

But back to 2016.

Things start out promisingly enough. First, I make the inspired (read foolish) decision to use a spice paste different from the one in the recipe. Why? Why would I do such a thing, you ask? Because I'd already made a general spice paste some weeks ago from a recipe from a Eurasian cookbook and I'd cleverly (or so I thought) made up a large batch of the generic rempah (onions, tumeric, garlic and chilli) and frozen it in jars. Little did I know, when I triumphantly unearthed one of these from the freezer (shortcut! domestic goddessness!) that the spice paste is entirely too orangey-yellow. That's what happens when there's way too much tumeric. This I know now.

After some hopeful and eventually desperate stirring over the flame, the curry gravy is a suspicious yellow-orange, nothing at all like the fire-red of my mother's. Any remaining hope is dashed when I taste a spoonful. Bitter. Almost like an aftertaste of Panadol. Even the chicken thighs and Unorthodox Ingredient No. 1: bacon (yes, the kind normal people eat for breakfast, because in the end, I couldn't find smoked ham bones at Cold Storage) I'd chucked in weren't masking the bitterness. I am forced to face the (bitter) truth. This so-called debal is in dire need of intervention. What's the opposite of bitter? Sweet! So I do what anyone who is forbidden refined sugar would do. Go to the fridge and get out Unorthodox Ingredient No. 2: Israeli Amary dates. After tossing in the first date, I realise that no one wants a mouthful of shard-like date skin pieces, so I peel and remove the seeds from three other dates then toss in the reddish-brown flesh.

Another taste. Better. No Panadoly aftertaste. But still none of the piquant tang of my mother's gravy. I am reluctant to pour in more vinegar than what the recipe called for; too much vinegar can taste really harsh. That's when inspiration for Unorthodox Ingredient No. 3 blossoms: tamarind. Who cares that I've committed enough sacrilege with bizarre ingredients to make long-departed grannies rise from the tomb?

Assam or tamarind fruit has less bite than vinegar, so it's a less risky option. It's funny though, that I'm even thinking in terms of 'risk' anymore. So in goes some assam pulp, softened with water, through a sieve. Another taste. Now there's that satisfying tang. Maybe it's my imagination, but it's starting to taste almost like my mother's.

I stare at the bubbling mixture. The chicken and bacon stare back at me. The colour is still not right – a half-hearted orange – but the taste is pretty much fine. But this brings me to a new problem.

When I started out, I wanted to cook this debal just for fun, but now that I've tasted it, all those Christmas smells and memories have come flooding back. I want to eat this thing – chicken chunks, streaky bacon and everything. Is it realistic for me to cook Eurasian food, which is generally meat-heavy, given my no-meat restrictions? Would I have to say goodbye to my own cuisine in this quest for health? And what about future Christmases? How was I going to survive sitting at the festive dinner table without keeling over from meat envy?

I yank myself back to my dilemma of the present. I stare at the chicken. The chicken stares back at me, as if saying, 'You know you want to. Go on then … bite me.'

Then, like dawn breaking over the horizon, epiphany comes. There is another way. To enjoy my debal and still keep to my new approach to eating. I open the cupboard. A flick of the wrist and the cans are yawning. Contents swished under running water then tossed into the steaming pot.

The Italian brown lentils and cannellini beans sink slowly into the bubbling liquid. I hover, damp with anxiety. What will finally emerge? A horrific Frankenstein? Or hopefully, something without screws sticking out of its head?

After some ineffectual stirring, I can't take it anymore. It's been over five minutes, the beans must have absorbed the flavour of the spiced gravy by now. I spoon out some, making sure to get a goodly amount of lentils and beans in the ladle.

Taste. Pause. Chew.

Pause.

Pause.

Pause.

Smile.

The Mosquito

It watched the first arrivals struggling to unload a piano from the lorry. They smelled of iron and driedsweat and pig. The mosquito watched as, day by day, the trees of the Malayan jungle were felled, roots attacked and burnt, branches piled high and set afire. One by one, the skeletons of huts rose and the community moved into these cubes of timber and attap.

There were a great many places to hide in these huts. The cool gaps between cupboards and walls, the corners of roofs, the dark underneaths of tables and chairs that were a respite from the afternoon swelter.

The humans toiled in the day, struggling to eke vegetables and grain from the yellow clayey soil.

'Ideal arable land my foot! The bloody Japanese really swindled us good and proper!' a man grumbled as he walked past the hut where the mosquito dozed.

It must be difficult, to have to labour so to fill their bellies. For the mosquito it was easy. It only had to follow the plumes of carbon dioxide and scent unfurling from the host. Then it would slide its proboscis into a capillary and suckle nourishment. How fragile these humans were; how precariously their supremacy hung in the balance.

* * *

It had all started with Bishop Adrian Deval's announcement at Saint Peter and Paul's Church. The Japanese occupiers were inviting Singaporean Eurasians and a few Chinese Catholics, as well as so-called 'neutrals' like the Swiss and Danes to resettle in Bahau, up in the western coastal state of Negri Sembilan in the Malayan peninsula. The invading force seemed to believe that setting up self-sufficient farming communities was not only possible, it would solve some of the problem of a population they could not feed. A group of Singaporean Chinese had already settled in Johore, in some jungle backwater called Endau.

Valentin Sequeira was intrigued. They had been subsisting on powdery rice and tapioca since the British had abandoned them over a year ago. But what did they know about farming? They were mostly clerks and administrators for European firms or the former colonial government. As superintendent of the MacRitchie Reservoir, patrolling its surrounding jungle for illegal loggers, Valentin was fitter than most, but he was no agriculturalist.

While the Bishop spoke, another advantage presented itself to the minds of the listeners. Anyone who volunteered would also be free from the ever-watchful gaze of the *kempetai*, the Japanese secret police. The Eurasian community were regarded British sympathisers. There were stories of how the Japanese torturers rammed bamboo shards underneath fingernails and set them aflame, how they pumped water into stomachs till the sacs burst. Just last week, they'd caught wind that Bertie Neubronner hadn't surrendered his radio and was listening to BBC broadcasts. Bertie still hadn't been heard of since he'd been bundled away to the *kempetai* headquarters at Stamford Road in broad daylight.

'Perhaps it will be fun,' murmured the man sitting on the pew next to Valentin. 'A tropical Eden.'

* * *

Hacking away at tree roots to clear the ground for planting under the broiling sun left every muscle in Valentin's body depleted at the end of the day. He had been part of the first batch of people – mostly single men – who had moved there in December 1943, just after Christmas, tasked to prepare the land before the others arrived.

Now, like the other two thousand in the Bahau Settlement, he was starting to realise how naive he'd been. The hill rice had sprouted encouragingly into a mist of green but, for some reason, shrivelled after two weeks. They had also planted red-skinned sweet potatoes, papayas and French beans, but these seedlings had been ravaged by caterpillar, locust and crow.

Some enterprising women refused to starve to death waiting for food to grow. From their meagre rations provided by the Japanese, they pooled handfuls of flour, spoonfuls of oil, and bartered for potatoes and spices with others in the settlement to make curry puffs to sell at Bahau town eight kilometres away. The first time Valentin rolled coriander and peppercorns on the *batu giling* borrowed from Mrs Hogan next door, the aroma took him back to his wife preparing curry keema. As he moved the granite rolling pin across the spices on the stone board, the first step in making the fried pastries with the curried potato filling, the motion calmed him. He noticed he'd become increasingly on edge in the recent weeks. He wondered what his six children were doing at this very moment. He hoped Patsy, his youngest at five, hadn't gallivanted out of their house again to the shop at the bottom of the hill. He'd only just managed to get there in time with his rifle that occasion she'd been intercepted by the illegal loggers.

* * *

'What's father doing now?' asked Patsy as her mother stood by the kitchen sink, skinning the tapioca that looked like pale, fat worms.

'Growing lots of food for us.' Mother sounded angry, and Patsy wondered if she had done something wrong she'd forgotten about. But her mother just began rinsing the vegetables without another word. Patsy reckoned it was probably her brother Charlie, the eldest, who had got up to some mischief as usual.

Dinner, Patsy guessed, would be tapioca. Since the grownups had started being scared all the time, they hardly ate rice any more. Mother would sometimes buy rice secretly from the people who set up stalls early in the morning along the road at the bottom of the hill, but this was mostly broken grains in some powdery stuff. Patsy didn't particularly like rice. She preferred noodles. They were much tastier, especially the fried noodles with prawns wrapped in a big beige leaf that didn't look like a leaf at all, that Father used to bring home as a treat. But even she missed rice now.

'When is he coming back, Mother? And when will he take us to Bau-hau with him?'

'Go and wash your hands. Dinner will be ready soon.' Mother began slicing the tapioca on the wooden cutting board. Patsy stood there with her hands behind her back, waiting for Mother to answer her question, or at least look at her and smile in that friendly way she did when she used to cook the grated tapioca cake with sugar and coconut for them to take on picnics, before the Japanese people had arrived. But she just kept on cutting and sliding the chunks into a bowl with the knife blade, as if Patsy weren't standing right in front of her. After a while, she realised Mother wasn't going to answer, so she wandered off to see what her sisters and brother were up to.

As she sat at the dining table later with her four sisters and brother, Patsy swallowed the grainy boiled tapioca and imagined the rice growing where Father was. Would it be right in their own garden, sprouting on bushes? Trees? No, she was quite sure rice grew from the ground, rather like grass. And there would be carrots and potatoes and tomatoes and cucumber and corn. Perhaps there would even be chickens. And goats! It would fun to have a pet goat. She was sure most children had pet goats in the countryside, in places like Bauhau. She smiled at her second eldest sister, Theresa, across the table. Theresa made a flared-nostril monster face back at her when Mother wasn't looking.

* * *

Night was when the mosquito revelled in the glory of its kingdom. How laughable to hear them cry out in their sleep or in the throes of lovemaking as it slipped through the fissures of the netting, circling ears and faces in a taunting dance. The invincible humans, reduced to swearing impotence. Then it would retreat, allowing them a deceptive sense of relief. From the opposite direction, a second approach, silent this time, towards the exposed toe or thigh. With the bloodmeal settling warm in its stomach, the mosquito often liked to try for one final buzz around the face, until the victim jerked up in bed, swatting and shouting like a madman.

* * *

'What's this?' asked John. 'Didn't know you were so good at women's work.'

Before Valentin could reply, eighteen-year-old John Cordeiro had snatched a curry puff from the enamel dish.

'*Rayu*! That's for selling!'

'But I'm hungry.' A spray of crumbs flew from John's mouth.

'Youngster making a nuisance of himself again?' Hubert Westerhout, limber-jointed for his sixty years, stepped into the hut the three men shared.

'Depleting the supplies, what else.' Valentin fished another curry puff out of the oil on the smoky wood fire contained in a clay bowl on wooden legs. He laid it on the dish.

Hubert's glasses flashed as he tricked the curry puff out of John's greasy fingers. 'Can't you make yourself useful, boy? We're winning the prize for worst farmers in history, you know.' He turned to Valentin. 'The other day you were telling me we're all going to die in this – what did you call it? – "this bloody sham of an Eden".' Hubert bit off a corner of plaited pastry and chewed. 'If I'm going to hell I might as well go there on a full stomach.'

* * *

Mrs Hogan's husband was the first person in the settlement to die of malaria. As the funeral service began, the setting sun cast emaciated fingers across the hill slope before them. The tiny community had no idea that until they boarded the first train back to Singapore after the Japanese surrender, the row of crosses would stretch from ten, to twenty, to fifty, until the wooden sticks marked over a quarter of their number.

Up in the rafters of the attap and bamboo hut where Valentin, Huber and John lived, the mosquito dozed.

***

That night, in the girls' large shared bed, Patsy's sisters Theresa and Emily were whispering.

'*Yo jah drumi kon gatu. Jah murdeh na ku,*' they chanted the words of the rhyme, giggling at the idea of the house cat biting their bottoms.

'Father said we're not supposed to speak Kristang,' scolded Margaret, the eldest.

'Father isn't here,' said Therese.

Patsy's whisper was fierce. 'But he's coming back.'

The movement across the bed subsided and a hush crept over the girls.

'Well,' said Margaret, clasping her hands over the rag doll on her chest in a prim posture, 'goodnight.'

Patsy turned to face the window so her eldest sister

wouldn't hear her. '*Bong anoti* Papa,' she whispered. She thought about how during the day, the forest outside was full of shadows but at least there were some cracks where the light tumbled through. Night was when the trees merged into a terrifying wall of darkness.

* * *

John stared at Hubert lying on the bed. 'What's wrong with him?'

'I don't know. He's been shivering and saying he's been feeling cold since last night. Now he's burning up.'

Hubert turned his flushed face toward Valentin and John. His cheeks and forehead were shining with damp. 'Stop fussing like two old ladies, both of you. Go and see to the long beans. They're not going to water themselves, you know.'

Valentin and John exchanged looks. After a few seconds, John said under his breath, 'You heard we're out of nails? Brother Herman was asking you to come by to talk about supplies.'

'Okay. I'll just sit with him a few more minutes, in case he needs anything.'

Giving Hubert an uncertain glance, John shrugged then went out of the hut. When Hubert seemed to have drifted off to sleep, Valentin went over to the box under his bed and took out the wooden figure he'd been working on. Resuming his seat by Huber's bed, he began whittling.

'Val!' Hubert started. He let out a high-pitched scream.

'What? What is it?' Valentin bent over him and tried mopping his brow with a wet twist of rag.

Hubert shoved his hand away with the strength of a man half his age. He shuddered a sigh then his tone gentled. 'Ah, Rosie. As beautiful as she was on our wedding day.' His eyes glazed into the distance, out the window. 'She loved that silk camellia, you know. Wore in her hair for special occasions. I saved up for two months to buy it from Whiteaway.'

Valentin glanced in the direction where Hubert's blood-shot eyes were fixed, but in the frame was only the usual square of lalang waving in the breeze.

* * *

For two whole weeks before she turned six, Patsy prayed every night before bed that her father would return and take them to Bau-hau. On the morning of her birthday, they were seated at the dining table. She knew there would be little chance of a birthday cake, and she didn't know what exactly she'd been hoping for but she couldn't help feeling slightly disappointed when she saw only the usual boiled tapioca for breakfast. Then she happened to look out the window. A dark shadow was making its way through the jungle beyond the compound.

Before Mother could stop her, she pelted out of the house and ran down the driveway. She leapt into his arms.

'Father! I knew you'd come!'

'I'm in Singapore to buy nails. And for your birthday, of course. Here, I made something for you.'

Father reached into his pocket and pulled out a wooden doll. Patsy squealed and hopped around in circles. 'What's her name? What's her name?'

'That's up to you.'

'Bunky.'

'Bunky? That's an unusual name! And what does "Bunky" mean?'

Patsy giggled. 'She likes bunnies and monkeys like me, so her name is Bunky!'

Father laughed. 'That's a very good name in that case.' He picked her up easily and as he carried her along the driveway to the house, he began to tell her a new story. There was a magical tree that grew all sorts of food – roast chicken, ham, curry, fruit, cake. 'Imagine, like a Christmas tree and gingerbread house put together. You can pluck off the decorations like roast chicken and eat them!'

'Did you bring us any?'

'Of course not!'

'But why?'

'Because if I did then you wouldn't come and visit me in

Bahau, would you?'

'No, no, I'll go, I promise. Even if there's no roast chicken tree. Can I go with you to Bau-hau, Father? Please? On the train?'

Father paused mid-stride and looked like he was considering it. Then he shook his head. 'No.' His face was solemn.

'But why? Please, Father? I promise I'll be good.'

'Because I know a faster way.' He scooped her up and pretended to toss her in the air. 'We'll fly!'

Later that evening, as a birthday treat, Patsy got to go with Father and Mother all the way into town, to the grand Tanjong Pagar railway station. They waited at the platform, crowded with people. Some were carrying cloth bundles on their heads, others lugged worn suitcases. They all looked like they were in a great hurry and would be very annoyed if anyone stopped them for any reason. Patsy kept a tight hold of Bunky in one hand and of Father's hand in the other. As the nose of the train slowed along the platform with a screech, the excitement she had felt earlier about being the special one allowed to see him off had faded.

'Don't go, Father! Take me with you, please, I promise I'll be good!'

Father squatted so he looked her straight in the eyes. 'Patsy, you must be patient. You're a big girl now, six years old. Before your next birthday, all of us will be in Bahau together.'

'Promise?'

'Of course I promise.' He wrapped his arms around her and kissed the top of her head. At that moment, Patsy believed him.

Back in Bahau later that day, John leaned on his shovel and slid the back of his forearm across his brow. 'Do you think that's deep enough?'

Valentin regarded the hole in the ground. He had no idea. He had never dug a grave before.

Later, they buried Hubert Westerhout just as the sun was dipping over the edge of the hill and the crickets were beginning to chirp.

In Singapore that night, after her sisters had fallen asleep, Patsy crept out of bed and went to sit by the window. She held Bunky close. Through the blackness outside, she tried to make out the road leading from the house into the knotted tangle of forest, the road they had taken earlier that day, all the way to the railway station. She imagined the railway track that ran over the Causeway bridge into Malaya, up, up and up until it reached Bau-hau, where Father was preparing a place for all of them.

In Bahau that same night, as Valentin Sequeira lay in deep slumber, the mosquito circled his ear. He smelled of dried sweat and underneath that, the perfumed cake humans washed themselves with. The mosquito hovered out of the reach of swatting hands and settled on his inner ankle, gleeful in the knowledge that the negligible weight of its body didn't register on the human epidermis. Its proboscis pierced the skin. The surge of fluid into its belly sent it to ecstasy.

Pineapple Tarts, Angklongs and Homemade Monopoly

AS TOLD TO MELISSA DE SILVA BY KERRY KESSLER, WHOSE LATE GRANDMOTHER, JANE SPYKERMAN NEE PINTO, WAS SISTERS WITH NELLIE PINTO (MOTHER OF MELISSA'S MATERNAL GRANDFATHER CYRIL PINTO)

It would appear that spending a night in a cemetery was some kind of rite of passage for Eurasian boys. I recall my cousins recounting similar tales. I have two crazy cousins who actually did spend an entire night in Bidadari … However, they both had different versions of who almost wet his pants!

My grandmother spoke little English and in the beginning we spoke little Kristang but we understood the other's language over time, even if neither attempted to speak it much. The only time I remember my grandmother speaking English was to reprimand us for infractions invariably committed by my older male cousins. The little ones were just caught in the crossfire. It was then that she would surprise us with her command of the English language. Grandma was fierce when she was riled up, and nothing riled my grandmother as much as having someone mess up her kitchen or having her meatsafe raided at all hours of the night. It didn't help that my cousins were constantly hungry, being the growing teenage boys that they were.

We were a large family – my mother and her young family (six of us) and her oldest sister Freda and her family of ten (parents included) all lived together with my grandmother in her three-bedroom house in Serangoon Gardens. My cousins and I played outdoors a lot. Money was tight but we never wanted for anything. We were creative little kids and we made a lot of our toys from discarded stuff we found around the home. I still remember the go-kart my older cousins made from wooden crates they salvaged from the local fruit seller. Three or four little boy cousins would pile into this makeshift go-kart (brakeless no less) and come careening down a steep hill close to grandma's house. Thankfully no one came home with any broken bones, although there were a lot of bruised little bodies, some bruised egos, as well as a couple of suitably chastened older brothers. One of my more musically inclined cousins dedicated a good part of his afterschool hours to making a guitar, which he and his brothers taught themselves to play. Then there was the 36x36-inch Monopoly board fashioned from vanguard sheet, glued on plywood duplicated from the original board game, which if I remember correctly, was one of our neighbours' discards.

We loved having visitors and we used to get a lot as Grandma had five other children with several children of their own as well as numerous nephews and nieces, the children of her sisters Nellie and Daphne, as well as her adopted brother Edward. Christmas at Grandma's house was an unending parade of visitors as they came to pay their respects to Grandma and to enjoy her famous bajek and dodol, which she made over an angklong, an outdoor stone oven. I have to say, my grandmother's pineapple tarts were a hit and miss. She never baked from a recipe so we never knew how the pineapple tarts would turn out each year, although she would swear it was better than the last. I only remember all the aunts and girl cousins sitting around the back patio, each focused on her particular task in the tart making assembly line, all the while the older family members would talk and laugh. There was a lot of laughing. I felt really sorry for the aunt given the unfortunate task of scraping off the burnt out bottoms of the tarts from the baking sheets in preparation for the next batch of cookies to go into the oven! To this day, every year when my mom and I make our tarts, we would reminisce about those days as we marvel how easily our tarts slide off these new- fangled non-stick cookie sheets. My grandmother would have been proud of how far we had come at improving the look and taste of her pineapple tarts.

To understand how the Kristang language and culture was

passed down in previous generations, you have to understand how life was back then for us. Growing up in the early 1960s, we didn't have much in the way of luxuries like a television, a telephone or even a camera. Granted, those items were not ubiquitous back then, but for us it was mostly because money was scarce. Life was simple and families spent a lot of quality time together where we actually talked to each other. Okay, so the adults talked and being the nosey kids that we were, we tried to surreptitiously follow the adult conversations being spoken in Kristang. Those were the days when children were to be seen but not heard, but thankfully my aunts and uncles were a progressive lot. They enjoyed our company as much as we enjoyed theirs, and they loved sharing their experiences growing up in rural Singapore. They would regale us with stories of life in the Woodbridge Mental Hospital quarters, where they lived until my grandfather retired, their interactions with the residents of the hospital, about the war and how the family got through it with the virtues of their six teenaged daughters intact, as well as hair-raising ghostly encounters in the surrounding kampongs.

Can't vouch for the veracity of some of those ghost stories but we hung on to every word. A lot of the family history (some would call it gossip) and life lessons were passed on orally at family gatherings and we were a captive audience. My girl cousins and I were especially entertained by stories of the romantic overtures of the Eurasian boys in the neighbouring Catholic boys schools toward my aunts, and accounts of their subsequent dates. Back in those days a romantic date was dinner and a movie. Not much has changed except that, back then, girls and boys dressed up for the movies; girls in a party dress and boys in a shirt and tie. It all sounded so romantic!

I remember your great-grandmother Nellie Pinto visiting us every Christmas. She usually came alone and would stay for lunch before making the trek home again. She was a very petite, dark- complexioned woman who never spoke much, but was always quick with her smile. I was told that Aunty Nellie struggled after her first husband (your great-grandfather) died and life was hard but she always kept a scrupulously clean home and there was always food on the table. They would tell us she was so clean that she would remove the kapok filling of her pillows to air out in the sun while she washed the casings. I don't know why I remember that story, but for me she embodied a life lived with dignity in the face of extreme hardship. I can truly say that those life lessons learnt at family gatherings and stories of resiliency and faith in God when times were dark, helped shape my life and gave me the mettle to tackle some of the most difficult moments in my own life.

Eurasian Tea
is an Actual Thing

I'm not a big fan of raucous female-only parties where silly games are played and paper things worn on heads – hen nights, for one – and it was with some measure of trepidation that I rolled up to Nicole's home in a taxi that afternoon for a baby shower. I totally wanted to celebrate her upcoming baby – yay, new small gurgly thing – but preferably without a competitive element involving paper hats, diapers or pacifiers.

So it was with rapture and delight that what greeted me when I ventured into the dining room was … a tea spread. And not just any old tea spread, but one of quintessential Eurasianness. There was The Sugee Cake. Baked by Nicole's aunt, it was a three-tiered glory wrapped in blue, white and lilac fondant, proclaiming 'Boy, Oh Boy' (yes, it was a boy). It presided over the table on a porcelain cake stand. Flanking it were supporting-role brownies and pretty iced cupcakes made by other female relatives. There was an incarnation of the simple childhood dessert we used to love, tinned peaches drizzled with evaporated milk. This version took the form of a jelly cream-cloudy with evaporated milk, jewelled with peach slices. There was also mee goreng, spicy (but not the Indian coffee shop style that would dye your inner organs red). My gluten and dairy-free status had me sidestepping these delicacies. I gravitated towards a majestic kueh salat. The lower pulut layer was threaded with a reassuringly non-violent shade of blue. Probably real *bunga telang* had been used for the tint. The custard layer, a natural dull pandan green, was all eggy deliciousness and coconut milk bliss (miles apart from the commercial stuff thickened with cheaty corn starch or flour).

After I'd shamelessly monopolised the kueh salat, I spied another dish. A platter of mango and sliced pears. The indecent wetness of the mango was no obstacle to my greed. And the pears, which I usually consider a blah fruit, surprised me with a delicate perfume and flavour. All this indulgence was chased by a clean, clarifying black tea, served in gilt bone china that made this tea service fanatic swoon. I confess, I spend an unhealthy amount of time looking at teacups, saucers, pots and cake stands online.

It was only months later that Nicole made her own a confession to me – her family had a secret tea that hadn't been served that day. It was what they used to have at the weekly Sunday tea gatherings at her late grandmother's home at Jalan Bahagia, when she was alive. The secret starts with the tea bags. No Lipton. Use six to eight Marks & Spencer tea bags (preferably the Extra Strong variety in the blue box), and add boiling water to a large teapot. Then put the entire teapot into the microwave (yes, the microwave) for two to three minutes. So the tea steeps and boils again. Then add half a tin of condensed milk and some sugar. The result is a thick, frothy tea rather like teh tarik, or masala chai without the spices. The kids weren't allowed to drink the special tea, but would have Ribena, orange juice or water.

And of course there was the food. There would be French loaf with serikaya and Kraft cheese (important note: not together). The puddingish coconut and egg spread would be made by her grandmother, Anna Elizabeth Puspalm nee De Souza.

Serikaya is Portuguese in origin. The Portuguese are famed for their pastries, like the *pastel de nata* (known as the Portuguese egg tart, literally translated as pastry of cream), filled with a rich custard of milk, sugar and egg yolks. The Portuguese took their culinary pastry tradition with them to their colonies, leading to the presence of Portuguese egg tarts in Macau, Mozambique and Brazil. As for how all of this connects to serikaya, my guess is an enterprising local cook for a colonial Portuguese household in Goa or Malacca substituted the original cow's milk in a custard recipe with more affordable and easily available coconut milk. In those tropical monsoon lands, you couldn't throw a stone without hitting a coconut palm. Then somebody figured out the custard was amazing just on bread, sparing them the hassle of making all those pastry shells.

But back to Nicole's family tea. Somebody would bring a cake. And the fun would begin. When we meet at a café in Holland Village the week before she returns to work from maternity leave, Nicole tells me what the Eurasian tea ritual means to her: 'It's a time for the whole family to gather. The Chinese have their steamboat, where they gather for a communal meal. Eurasian tea is like that. Teatime on Sundays at my Grandma's place was when things were celebrated. Birthdays, anniversaries. We celebrated many anniversaries. At 2pm people would arrive and just hang out and relax and around 4pm we would have tea. We did this every week when my grandmother was alive.'

In my own family, my mother tells me how my grandmother would have a rotation of things for weekday tea. One thing she made, which my mother continued to make for tea when we were kids, was goreng kodok. The fitters of mashed banana, egg and flour would balloon up in the hot oil, and you'd be so eager to bite into them before they deflated you'd burn your greedy fingers. While they were frying, the aroma of burnt caramel from the sugar in the bananas would fill the entire home.

Like many Eurasians, my mother and her siblings would also have simple sandwiches for tea, like cucumber or cheese.

And the French loaf they would buy from the Indian bread man would star some days as well, slapped with margarine and brown kaya of dubious origin (that my mother insists they were grateful for). Bubur terigu, a porridge of white wheat sweetened with gula melaka, laced with coconut milk, was also a regular teatime feature, as in many other Eurasian homes. *Bubur* means porridge in Malay, and *terigu* is derived from the Portuguese word *trigo*, which means wheat. Some days there would be pulut hitam, black glutinous rice porridge, another typical Eurasian tea item. Often there would be some tapioca dish, sometimes grated with coconut and sugar. My maternal grandmother, Patsy Pinto, had seven children. So she cooked up vats of local ingredients which could be doled out to eternally hungry kids.

When I lived with her till I was five, it was the late 70s and early 80s. The epicurean landscape had shifted. Commercially made food was available and affordable. So some of my tea time favourites were Sara Lee butter cake and chocolate cake (the marble cake was neither here nor there). And of course, the ultimate winner was the gluttonous chocolate rice butter toast.

My other grandmother had an even bigger brood to feed. Twelve children. Even years later when all the kids were grown, she would still make teatime favourites like kueh salat and pulut inti. There would be bunga telang growing wild along the fence of my parents' old home in Jalan Tari Lilin.

When she visited she would harvest the blooms to make the kueh.

Some say the whole afternoon tea ritual by the Eurasian community was an affectation aping the English middle class, started during the colonial era. They believe these people wanted to adopt the cultural practices of the power elite. I've read of how some Eurasian families would dress up for tea, for example. Perhaps for these, the ritualistic element of the proper bone china tea service and the codified English-like behaviour surrounding it might have been. But I think it's reasonable to conclude that for many families, afternoon tea wasn't a matter of trying to adopt British behaviours. It likely boiled down to a very universal human concern – the rumbling of the tummy. If one has lunch at 1pm and dinner is at 7 or 8pm, what would have been more natural than a small snack and a cup of something hot to break the long stretch in between?

Eurasian tea was a thing mothers and grandmothers did with their children and grandchildren in the past. Today, most parents are at work in the afternoon, so a weekday family tea is out of the question. For some families, the tradition still survives, morphed into a weekend ritual, usually held at the nucleus of the family clan, the grandparents' home. And the heart of the gathering, besides the spread encompassing East and West, remains the typical Eurasian teasing and joking and close interaction between generations.

Some of my fondest family memories are of teatime and this is one tradition I intend to keep alive. Let the search for the perfect tea service begin.

How To: Belachan
and Chinchalok

As told to Melissa De Silva
by her father, Oliver De Silva

When I was a boy in upper primary, I would follow my mother to the Portuguese Settlement in Malacca during the school holidays. My grandfather, Peter Pereira (my mother's father and your great-grandfather) was a fisherman. He made his own fishing nets from nylon string. He would use this sort of instrument made of bamboo with a flap cut into the middle to weave the nets. It was the Portuguese-Eurasian fishermen who knew how to trawl for shrimp. They would use a very fine, triangular net called a *langgiang* in Kristang. It was as fine as mosquito net. The net had two wooden rollers that would move along the sea floor. Then they would wade knee deep through the water holding the *langgiang* to catch the shrimp.

One thing my grandfather taught me to make from the shrimp was chinchalok. First, get pink, fresh shrimp. Happy shrimp, he called it. About 250 grams. The pinker the better.

If you use fresh shrimp, your chinchalok won't spoil. Grey shrimp are no use. Grey means they are dead! Then you get an empty bottle with a screw cap, like a whisky bottle.

Pour in half a capful of brandy into the bottle and swirl it all around inside until the brandy covers the whole inner surface of the bottle. This is to kill the germs. Then you put the shrimp in the bottle. Don't wash the shrimp. The sea has already sterilised them. Then you add one tablespoon of cooked rice – the sugars in the rice help the shrimp to ferment – and one tablespoon or less of salt.

Screw the cap onto the bottle. Then you leave it in a cool place, like on the kitchen table. Leave it to ferment for a few days, up to one week. Every two or three days, turn the bottle up and down to distribute the salt. Sometimes what's at the bottom has fermented but not what's on top. So every other day or so, unscrew the cap to let the air out. Then you can move the bottle to mix it all up.

After a few days or a week, you can have a taste. Dip a clean chopstick into the chinchalok. Every time you taste, always use a different clean chopstick.

How you eat chinchalok is to serve it with red chilli. Crushed, bruised or sliced. Also chopped onion, and squeeze lime on it. If you eat it with asam pedas and rice, it's really shiok.

My grandfather also taught me how to make belachan. You

can use even 1kg of fresh, pink shrimp, because you can keep belachan in the fridge. Give the shrimp a brisk wash to remove any small particles, but you want to retain the salt from the sea water. Put it in the sun for a few days, covered with a basket to keep away the flies. When you see the volume of the shrimp gets less, and when it feels semi-dry, put it in a *batu tumbuk* and pound it until it becomes a paste.

Shape the paste into a balls or any other shape and leave them to dry in the sun again for about a week. Cover it with a basket for hygiene. Turn the belachan periodically. Do this during hot weather, it must be good, hot sun. When you feel a crust forms, break up each ball of belachan and reshape it to a new ball. This will thoroughly mix it up and produces the best belachan. It will smell like belachan when it's cured.

Keep it in a tight jar, but air the belachan from time to time or it will become watery. When you want to use it, toast it first.

But the thing is, where are you going to get fresh shrimp now? Last time you used to be able to get it at Punggol jetty, but now it's all gone, made way for condominiums. Even in Malacca you cannot get fresh shrimp any more.

Mother Tongue

We are studying *peribahasa*, idioms. There are many lists to learn in Malay, *seerti-seiras* (synonyms), *berlawan* (opposites) and *peribahasa*. In primary school, my favourite Malay idiom was *gajah berak besar, kancil pun mau berak besar.* The elephant takes a big crap, so the mousedeer wants to take a big crap too. Seriously. It's a cautionary statement about unrealistic aspirations. The other one I liked because of the absurd image: *burung terbang pipiskan lada.* To throw chilli at a bird in flight. The warning of not hurrying to take action until an event is certain. Some solid wisdom there.

Malay class at CHIJ Toa Payoh Primary was mostly made up of Eurasian girls who were terrible at Malay. A complete disinterest in the language might have had something to do with it. Out of the bunch of us, there were five actual Malay girls, a gravelly voiced girl with cat's eyes called Siti, tomboyish Azryn, another girl whose mother was a retired singer of 60s/ 70s fame, smiley Susie and tiny, perpetually scared-looking Kartini.

One highlight was enforced singing on Fridays. I have no recollection of this, but my good friend Emilie Oehlers assures me of every detail in astounding clarity. Apparently we were forced to go up in pairs to sing songs in front of the entire class. In Malay. Emilie says she and Nicole Batchelor would always go up together and sing '*Potong Bebek Angsa*' every Friday on repeat. Nicole recently sent me a link to the lyrics online and I managed to find an English translation. Now that I go over the lyrics as an adult, I realise the song is bizarrely macabre. It involves cutting up a goose, then for some reason, a dancing woman waltzes into the picture. It's no wonder I blocked it out. These are some of the lyrics:

Potong bebek angsa, masuk di kuali,
Nona minta dansa, dansa empat kali,
Dorong ke kiri, dorong ke kanan,
Tralala lala lala lala la la

This roughly translates to:

Cut the goose's breast, put it in the wok,
The lady asks for a dance, dance four times
Push to the left, push to the right
Tralala lala lala lala la la

Even now that I understand all the words, it still doesn't make sense to me. What's the relation between the woman and the goose? What's with the pushing to the left and the right? Goodness knows what song I went up to sing. Clearly,

I must have blocked out these happy events. Maybe I kept silent while my poor partner, whoever she was, did all the grunt work, or maybe I was sly enough to lip-synch.

Back then as a child, I never understood why I was studying Malay. Why go through all this torture? This is not my mother tongue, thank you very much, I would tell my *Cikgu* silently in my head. My mother told me our mother tongue was English, but that didn't seem right either. But more on that later. Now, in my thirties, I love the fact that I possess at least one Southeast Asian language, and shockingly, am at ease ordering nasi campur and kueh from a roadside warung in Malaysia. When I break out in my limited Malay vocab to taxi driver *enciks* across the Causeway, they look surprised when they hear I'm from Singapore. When I explain that I am Serani and I '*belajar Melayu di sekolah*', that I am Eurasian and I studied Malay at school, they nod and go 'Ah ... *bagus*.' In their eyes is something like approval, and perhaps I'm crazy, but also something like pride.

There is a Malay uncle assigned to clean my block, an adorable tiny man about five feet high. He has a face that reminds me of Popeye the sailor. The fact that he's always in a faded olive cap adds to the sailorish quality, even though this headgear in no way resembles Popeye's black and white skipper's hat. The uncle also doesn't smoke a pipe. Instead he has a wisp of a hand-rolled cigarette dangling permanently from his mouth as he goes about sweeping the void decks and the drainage indents along our corridors. Still, the distinct Popeye-ness is there. Whenever I leave the house in the morning and see him in the vicinity, I make it a point to slow down or adjust my path so it takes me closer to him, so he can see me. Then he will look up and his whole face lights with a gummy smile. And I'll try to get in a '*Selamat pagi*' before he does. Yes, I feel ridiculously pleased that I can do this. Once I even chanced upon him at the bus stop near my block, after he had finished work. And I did something I later laughed at myself for, for my sheer mad ambition. I went and sat next to him on the cement bench and tried to have a conversation with him. In Malay. Well, he spoke Malay and I kind of understood eighty percent of what he said. Mega achievement. I didn't speak very much back though. He told me he's assigned to a few blocks, what time he starts work each morning and that he ends at 3pm each day. Also that he has Sundays off. I don't know what he thinks I 'am', *orang Serani* or just someone who happens to be able to speak really bad Malay, but it doesn't matter. Just being able to have that exchange at the bus stop as the six lanes of traffic roared by, was a testament to human affinity with this man who until then had hovered at the edge of my existence each day (except Sundays). All made possible by those Malay classes taken so very long ago.

But when I was a child, I hated the mandatory lessons that seemed to have nothing to do with me. The first week of primary school, I confronted my mother. The conversation between my seven-year-old self and my exasperated mother went something like this:

'Mummy, what's our mother tongue?'

'English.'

'Then why am I taking Malay in school?'

'Because it's easier than Tamil or Chinese.'

'Why would I be taking Tamil or Chinese?'

'It's just easier. You want to learn Chinese or Tamil characters, is it?'

'No, but we are not Malay what. Why do I have to take Malay if I'm already studying English?'

'It's just the rules of school.'

'They said in secondary school we can choose Spanish or French or German.'

'So?'

'Can I take Spanish?'

Later, I was to discover that Malay would be one of my threads of cultural inheritance, not by any specific ancestor I could trace and name, but through reasonable assumption. Since the Portuguese colonised Malacca and intermarried with local women, some of them would certainly have been Malay. I believe it's safe to assume that I have at least some Malay heritage. So those Malay lessons were not irrelevant to my existence after all. In time, I came to see them as an enriching opportunity to experience another language and culture I would otherwise never have had access to.

Fast forward to 2016. I have been attending mother tongue lessons of a very different sort. These are of my own volition, and conducted by a teacher much younger than myself. The most significant point though, is that for the first time in my life, I am formally learning my mother tongue. Which is *not* English.

Of course, Kristang, being a creole of Portuguese and Malay, isn't every Singaporean Eurasian's mother tongue. Eurasians of other threads of heritage may count many other languages – German, Khmer, Thai, French, for example – among their wealth of mother tongue inheritance. But since my four grandparents all were of Portuguese-Eurasian heritage (my maternal grandmother's maiden name was Sequeira, my maternal grandfather was a Pinto, my paternal grandfather a De Silva, and my paternal grandmother's family name was Pereira), for me Kristang is truly my mother tongue.

The course is conducted by linguistics student Kevin Martens Wong, whose mother is Eurasian. The linguistic wonder basically learned Kristang on his own by reading up and memorising the scant available material, such as a handful of dictionaries and a few books and poetry collections written by a Kristang activist in Malaysia by the name of Joan Marbeck.

There is no socialist regime enforced public singing.

Instead, we play games, which are pleasantly trauma-free. One lesson, we played a game called Mar di Rikeza (Sea of Riches).

This sprang from the brain of Martens Wong. The objective was to get us used to the names of the cardinal points and colours. A map of the Bijagos Archipelago, off the coast of Guinea-Bissau (another former Portuguese colony in West Africa) was projected on the wall. The Bijagos Archipelago is a modern-day smugglers' hideout, complete with drug cartels. Really. So, naturally, our goal was to look for treasure. Each of us was represented by a ship on the map. We would have to call out in Kristang where we wanted our ships to move – north-northeast, for example. If your ship happened to pass over a coordinate where treasure was hidden, it was yours. The treasures were romantic and colourful – the *Spada di Floris* (Sword of Flowers), *Korsang Jambu* (Pink Heart), the *Diamanti Azul* (Blue Diamond). But the life of a mariner is never plain sailing. We also had 'pirates' on our tails, other students and our other teacher Mr Bernard Mesenas, an elderly gentleman. They had the power to snuff out our lives. Exciting times.

For the first time since primary school, I have made a group of Eurasian friends – mother and daughter Mary and Eleanor Thomas, Kevin Michael Sim and Sharlene Pereira. And I mean friends, not just classmates. We hang out together after the Saturday morning lessons at NUS, and we've gone to the same restaurant for lunch in Holland Village so many times after class that we've been rewarded with a free round of chocolatey desserts by the wait staff. My friends' reasons for learning Kristang overlap with mine. Kevin Michael Sim thinks of it as 'his grandmother's tongue' and Eleanor wants to speak it to her own family one day. It makes Mary feel more connected to her ancestors.

Being able to speak in simple Kristang with them makes me feel more Eurasian. And I am beginning to feel like I have more of my own culture, which I've never felt like I had very much of, since I was a child. We Eurasians do not have many visible, tangible traits to point at and go 'Ta da! Culture!' We cannot boast of having unique beaded slippers, say, like the Peranakans, or a legacy of dynastic culture like the Chinese, or a wealth of literature, art and song like those from the Indian subcontinent. But what we do have, besides our awesome Eurasian cuisine, is this language, which is truly ours.

A few lessons into the Kristang course, I came across a quote by Nelson Mandela:

'*When you speak to man in a language he understands, he understands you with his head. When you speak to him in his mother tongue, he understands you with his heart.*'

A few months earlier, I wouldn't have understood what he meant, not truly. But after tasting my own language, I do. Now I am beginning to understand that a mother tongue is the language that speaks to the deepest part of a person's heart. It is the framework that shapes our worldview and articulates our physical, emotional and spiritual being. Possessing a tiny bit of Kristang – a treasure that grows with each lesson – gives me a feeling of stepping into a new world, a world that belonged to me all along, but now, finally, I have the key.

Letter to Anonymous Policy Maker (Re: 'Others' is Not a Race)

'Others' it said on the form. She considered that for a moment. What did 'Others' mean? 'Others' from whose point of view? As if some were conferred insider status and some not, 'the others'?

Using the pen chained to the counter with pink raffia string, she crossed out 'Others' and scratched in 'Eurasian'. After filling in the rest of the form, she tossed it into the tray on the counter and stalked out. Past the rows and rows of plastic chairs immobilised to the floor, past the electronic board summoning one string of numbers after the other in panicky staccato.

That evening, she sat down to beef hor fun in a takeaway paper box lined with a plastic sheet. She was only half paying attention to the TV as she chopsticked the slithery noodles into her mouth. The newscaster's voice announced the release of the PSLE results earlier that morning. Cut to the education minister outside a community centre, people in white and red uniform tees milling in the background. 'Overall, we are quite pleased with the performance this year. The Chinese have done well, showing improvements in all subjects, except mother tongue. We are investigating the situation further. The Malays also showed good improvement, especially in Maths. We believe this is the result of the support systems we have put in place. The Indians scored very well in English. We are looking into a possible buddy system to pair Indian students with their counterparts from other races. As for the Others ...'

There it was again.

The Others.

Who determined which people were 'others' and which people weren't? Just because there were fewer of them, did that mean they counted for less? Come on, they had been there since the beginning. Except for the original Temasek-dwellers. But since the first unions between the Portuguese and the Asians in Malaya in the 1500s.

There were many Eurasians in colonial times and after independence who had contributed to the development of the country too. Yet it was as if they'd been obscured from the official narrative. After decades of working together, building and living side by side, did it come down to this? Six meaningless letters on a form?

Others.

What does it mean, she wondered, when policy makers wilfully choose to see some within society as 'other'? As people on the outside, as if they were invisible? Many Singaporeans were ignorant that they were even fellow citizens. She recalled reading an article online, '7 Things We Can All Learn from Joseph Schooling's Olympic Win'. Something like that. And number seven was: 'Eurasians are born and bred Singaporeans too.'

Wow.

Seriously?

Like it was some kind of revelation.

Why the ignorance? It was obvious. It was the Chinese, Malays and Indians who were mentioned (in that order) at every official speech involving national policy matters. And 'Others', they were mentioned too, last. And most Singaporeans had no idea who or what these 'Others' were. And who could blame them, with such a foggy term? And so the perception that Singapore is only made up of Chinese, Malays and Indians is reinforced over and over again, with each policy speech, each flourish of government data, effectively conditioning a nation.

Naming, she reflected, confers a sense of identity. To leave someone unnamed – the unwanted infant, the runt of the litter – marks it for a life of inconsequence.

The newscaster droned on. From the neighbour's flat, the opening theme of the news in Mandarin wafted through the grilled windows. So they'd be hearing about the PSLE breakdown too, and the 'Others', just in another language.

It couldn't be a simple matter of people not knowing what a Eurasian was.

European + Asian = Eurasian.

Surely that wasn't too taxing on the brain? No, it seemed a wilful act of unacknowledgement. Whatever protests made to the contrary, justifying it as mere semantics for bureaucratic convenience. Naming, or leaving something unnamed, carries the weight of a lifetime of validation, or the withholding of such. Fuck this shit, she thought. She zapped off the TV.

Tossed the empty box down the chute. Went to her bedroom, pulled out her laptop and flopped down on her stomach in bed. She began to type:

TO: the anonymous policy maker
RE: 'Others' is not a race

Eurasian.
E-U-R-A-S-I-A-N.

Just because there are fewer of us, do you think we do not count?

Who are you to strip us of our identity?
Who are you to white out our name?

We are as Singaporean as you.

We came on the ships bearing Anglo-Indians
employed by the East India Company.
Yes, those were Eurasians.
We were here when they carved out the roads in the
wild days of the land,
washing gravel over red soil.
Norris, D'Almeida, Galistan.
The days of the British found us clerks and bailiffs,
engineers and storekeepers, forest rangers and
foremen.
And we were here too when the Japanese came
flooding, squat-looking insects, absurd high socks on
bicycles.
We had radios confiscated, were forced to bow, feel
the knife fear in our gut whenever we passed a khaki
soldier in the street,
Did we not die coaxing tapioca from unyielding
lands?
And we were here too when he cried on TV,
And wondered what the days to come would hold.

So, please do not give us any bullshit
about how it is 'a practical impossibility'
to capture any Singaporean's individual diversity.

Thank you, that is no news.
Yes this one comes from Fujian with Hokkien and
Mongolian ancestry.
And this one has great-greats from Java, and Bugis
with some Arab.
And this one is part Tamil, but also had an ancient
who was Malayalee.
Well and good and so they may be.
Yet they are graced with larger umbrellas that speak
mostly the truth
of who and what they are.
They are named.
Acknowledged.
They belong.
Not so of us, in your eyes.
Not enough to justify our own tickable box.
Boxes you believe so critical.

Others.
O-T-H-E-R-S

Are you so myopic, so lacking in human insight
and EQ,
that you do not see how insulting, how demeaning is
this label you've shrugged up?

Are you not able to – or perhaps you are simply
unwilling – to stretch your imagination to find a
better solution, a human solution,
that does not deny an entire people their cultural
identity?
No doubt your work is easier,
Of that I have no doubt
But do you not see the grave injustice?
A people who gave this country a president, a
cultural medallion winner,
an Olympic gold?
And even if we had not done these things,
It matters not.
We deserve to have our identity spoken forth
The word 'Eurasian' ribboning into the public
sphere In newsprint, public announcements,
To be heard and breathed, assimilated by all.
Can you not see how shoving an entire people into a
box with the sticker 'Others'
divorces them from everyone else,
draws a steel line in the sand?

Are Eurasians Singaporeans?
Singaporeans ask this
Singaporeans.
Ask.

This.

How is it that 198 years after Raffles landed, 52
years after we became a nation, such ignorance still
breeds?
This is the price of your administrative convenience.
The fruit of your tidy solution: 'Others'.

We are Singaporeans
And we are Eurasian too.
We belong and we deserve rightfully to be named.
So dear anonymous policy maker, hear me loud and
clear:
'Others' is not a race.

Blind Date

Martin Desker's surname had long been associated with a street of ill repute in Singapore's Little India. Nonetheless, he was proud of it. His name, that is. Even though he was no relation, Andre Filipe Desker, whom the road was named after, had been a man of Dutch descent, a Eurasian philanthropist of the 1800s.

Martin adjusted his walking stick against the marble-topped table once more.

Ten minutes to three.

The fruity, bitter fragrance of coffee was comforting. It was one of those time warp places designed to resurrect the 1990s, an era decades before he was born. The white interior calmed him. He ignored the walls implanted with screens that flickered to life with episodes of the quaint entertainment of the time, like *The Simpsons, Seinfeld* and *Baywatch*, depending on where you fell in the demographic. He'd chosen the place because instead of those glitchy holograms, there were proper human staff to take your order. He looked out the café window. The mechanical arms of the landscape bots snipped away at the unruly bits of pong pong lining the elevated cycle-ways. Smooth globes of tree emerged like sculptures under the effortless industry of the automated shears. It was all very impressive, but he often felt humanity had become obscured by these wonderful technological doodahs. Even the two coffees he'd ordered over the past hour had come with sugar molecules in a steel vial. You were supposed to spray it into your drink and escape with zero calories. He'd had ask for real sugar. Nonsense. Metal. What on earth was wrong with glass? Or wood? Surely anyone would prefer beautiful grain that told the life story of a tree? But of course, anything made from natural timber these days would cost the earth.

'Would you like another, sir?'

The waitress bent toward him as she spoke. Martin was startled by the reflection of his own bristly eyebrows in her irises that were exploding emerald fireworks. Another strange fashion. The other day he'd been standing across from a teenage boy on the subterranean tram. He couldn't put his finger on what was odd about the fellow until he realised his irises were miniature throbbing human hearts, complete with valves and everything.

'Sir?' She enunciated the word slowly, with a smile, as if he were an infant. People did that now. The more irritating ones would raise their voices, as if he were deaf. Idiots.

The café door jangled.

'No.' Dismissing her with a wave, Martin turned his stiff neck as far as he dared.

A woman of about thirty sloped in. She was wearing

one of those banned outfits that protected the wearer from surveillance. As she moved into the range of the café's monitoring system, her dress morphed through a sequence of shapes while emitting rapid bursts of light to throw off the camera's exposure calibration. Martin turned away.

Six minutes to three.

As another waitress whisked by the table, his walking stick threatened to collapse from the quiver of air as she passed. Reaching out to steady it, he caught a silvery outline at the window.

His heart began beating faster.

She entered the room like a ship bearing the face of Helen of Troy. Martin's fingers crept to his collar and he dabbed at the corner of his mouth. He laid down his napkin.

'My dear!' exclaimed the silver-haired vision.

Her eyes made deep crinkles as her gaze swept him up into itself. Then travelled to rest on a point behind him. Martin craned his neck the other way. A woman in black hulked at the bar, tracing her finger around the rim of a beaker of wine. Her eyes glowered up. The halo shimmered across the room. Cheeks kissed.

Martin turned away again. He couldn't decide if he were disappointed or relieved.

Four minutes to three.

The usual mix of 1990s English songs gave way to an even more ancient Mandarin one, old even in his parents' day. He didn't understand most of the words but he'd always felt the ache as the Taiwanese chanteuse compared her love to the moon. But they'd done something to it. The accompaniment had a flinty quality, like an electronic zither.

Martin swirled the dregs of his coffee. Ever since the last of his three sisters had passed away two years ago, he'd begun to search faces, as he walked down the street, wandered along grocery aisles or rode the tram. He'd also begun to miss words, words he wasn't sure he'd ever known. Try as he might, he hadn't been able to shake off the suspicion that 'heritage Eurasians' were on the brink of extinction. It was his own term for people like himself, people who counted both Asians and Europeans as their ancestors, an aberration of a community that was the particular outcome of unions in colonial days, now only a sepia haze.

In his parents' time, they'd already comprised less than one percent of the population. Each time he'd returned home from his postings at sea, there seemed to be fewer of them. He remembered how, growing up, his parents would make dinner table jokes about how their kind would soon vanish like the vaquita had, as the few Eurasians left kept marrying into other cultures. Later, he began thinking it wasn't so much like a species dying of extinction. It was more like a drop of ink dissolving into a bowl of water. Slowly, the tendrils of pigment would fade and blend into the larger body, until finally, there would be no evidence the original colour ever existed. All memory of them would be blurred away, and the Singaporeans remaining would be free of an uncomfortable reminder of a time when Europeans had crowed at the top of the social ladder, and the Asians, indigenous to Singapore as well as the settlers from China, India and the Indonesian archipelago, had allowed themselves to be 'ruled'.

After he'd returned home to retire a decade ago, he hadn't seen any Eurasians at all. If he spotted a suspected Eurasian on the street, he would scramble to approach them. It was ludicrous, he knew. But those moments had only happened six times in the past ten years. And he had never been right once.

It was not like being at sea. There was equilibrium in that solitude, the tranquility of being a silent spectator on the deck, in communion with the glories of nature. He drew it up again – always hovering just behind his eyelids – the Pacific at night. Crushed sky diamonds making dorsal fins glow in the oily black.

Why was it so different with faces? He would be lying in bed waiting for sleep or sitting on the balcony. As he scratched the top of Rufus' sandy head, he would watch the evening smog creep its charcoal fingers around the vegetation platforms dotting the tropical island. And his mind would reach for the faces of his mother and father and sisters. But nothing came. Of course there were pictures. But it was shocking his memory held no permanent impressions. The contours of their cheeks, the gullies running alongside the mouth, how could all these blur into a massive brown-beige vague? Obscure relics, like those old- fashioned graphite sketches, smudged with a thumb.

His walking stick clattered, jerking his eyes open. Before he could react, the waitress tripped over it, her back curving like an animation. The tray she was carrying sailed in the air.

Clang.

Latte waterfalls splashed. Martin half-rose to steady her. As he released his grip, someone tapped his shoulder. He turned round.

The man's head looked like a groundnut. His spectacles were foggy and the lower corner of the left lens was marked with a fingerprint. But something else hit Martin like lightning in the stomach.

'Excuse me, are you – ?' the man halted. His spectacles seemed to fog up even further from apparent embarrassment. 'Are you – Martin Desker?'

Martin nodded, mute. He tried to stand, feeling the creak in his knees. Reaching into his shirt pocket, he drew out a thin silicone rod and tapped one end of it with his index finger. It ejected a transparent, pliable sheet, as thin as paper used to be. As he laid it on the table, the sheet came to life with a moving graphic of the latest population census report, in the news two weeks ago. Among the rows of numbers for the various ethnic communities, circled in red, was the line:

ETHNIC ORIGIN: EURASIAN – POPULATION: 2.

When he tapped the rod again, the census report was replaced with an image of an advertisement:

EURASIAN MAN MARTIN DESKER SEEKS TO MEET
OTHER REMAINING EURASIAN IN SINGAPORE.
WILL BE WAITING AT CAFÉ BELVEDERE AT
96 WATERLOO STREET, 25 APRIL, 3PM.

Martin refocused on the man. When it came out, the report had confirmed his premonition. The next day, he'd placed the ad. After that, he'd been having the same dream every night.

He was at the Belvedere. He hadn't had coffee so his bladder was behaving. His dream self began to realise something was strange when a figure materialised at the door, silhouetted against the sunset. But it was only mid-afteroon so he didn't understand how there could be a sunset. Before the dream Martin could give this further thought, the figure grabbed his hand. A surge ran through him.

Martin was sailing again. From the deck, looking up at the blazing night sky, he was seized by the feeling that he was one of those stars, winging through the nebula. No longer was he a lone amorphous shape, adrift in the bucket of humanity.

Then he was a child again, standing beside his red plastic pail on Changi beach, toes squirming in sand that smelled of sun, invisible insects making his shoulders sting. And he'd found, in the microcosmic slop of ocean within the red walls, a miracle. A shape like himself.

He scooped it out carefully. Cradled the wet glistening in his palm, conscious of his heart pounding like a thousand galloping horses.

And conviction settled. It was as certain as existence, this graspable, tangible thing weighting his hand. It had a shape, distinct and knowable. It was real, and so was he.

'You're Martin Desker?' The man's voice ended in a tremulous quaver, bringing him back.

'Yes.' Martin's voice sounded remote, as if it had travelled an age through a yawning tunnel. 'That's me.' He paused then added, almost as if to himself, to confirm his identity, 'Martin Desker.' He put out his hand. 'Nice to meet you – ?'

The man's spectacles seemed to clear. Martin was caught off guard by the fleshy warmth of the palm.

'Gerald. Gerald Pereira.'

As the man pumped his hand, Martin savoured the music of that Portuguese surname. Pereira. So many Singaporean-Eurasians, no matter what their tapestry of heritage, could trace some ancestry to the former Portuguese presence in Malacca in the 1500s, and to Goa in India. It was absurd how giddy he felt encountering this stranger. Fragments from his childhood and memories that had been stored and carefully shaken out by his parents and grandparents rushed at him. Sambal sandwiches at funerals, jumping up at weddings to dance with sprightly grannies and aunties to '*Jinkli Nona*', as the Portuguese creole song told the tale of the man who desired to wed, open house the entire day after Midnight Mass on Christmas Eve, as visiting hordes of family and friends descended upon shepherd's pie and debal curry, the familiar inflections of their speech, that comfortable social openness that crossed boundaries unseen, unfelt, that familiar, easy warmth. It was so bizarre, yet it also felt perfectly natural that this man shared more with him than anyone else in this now alien land.

Martin noticed the eyes behind the spectacles. There was nothing foggy about them. They were a deep chestnut, flecked with copper, alive.

He renewed his grip. 'Gerald, you won't believe how happy I am to meet you.'

They take a slow walk from the café to the breathing dome at Fort Canning. Seated on a stone bench under the shade of a kranji tree, their feet dipped in the feeble sun, they embark on the Eurasian ritual, asking about family names, tracing backward into the past to see if their families are related. The roots appear to turn up a dead end and the two men settle on watching the traffic on the crisscrossing cycleways beyond the soaring crystalline dome.

'So,' Martin says, 'Did you find it strange I wanted to meet?'

Gerald laughs. 'Of course not. But I did wonder if this guy would be one foot in the grave already, like me.'

'I'm seventy-five. You mentioned you're sixty-six, right? So I'm the one nearer the grave.'

Gerald smiles. 'Not yet, not yet.'

Another easy silence settles between them. There's a sudden movement in the foliage of the rambutan tree across from their bench. A vermillion bird with a dark tail becomes visible through the leaves, dipping its beak into the plumage of its wing. The cool female voice of the audio commentary intones, 'Raffles' Malkoha. *Phaenicophaeus chlorophaeus.* This bird was a member of the cuckoo family. They built their nests high in rainforest trees.'

'So, did you have any siblings?' asks Martin, turning away from the hologram.

'Yeah, one brother. But he passed away. He was young, only in his forties. Heart attack. I don't know how it happened. He was always healthier than me. Didn't even drink.'

'He wasn't married?'

'No. What about you?'

'Three sisters. Lily married but never had any kids. Noisy money suckers, she used to say. Sophie and Emma never did. They lived together in my parents' home and passed away within a few months of each other, four years ago.'

'I'm sorry.'

'Thank you. They're in a better place now. Well, that's what I believe anyway. I'll show you a picture.'

Martin takes out his electronic screen and its pliable surface flickers to life.

Gerald nods as he surveys the image of the children at the beach. 'So nice we could still go swimming in the sea in those days.'

It might be his imagination, but it seems to Martin Gerald's spectacles mist up slightly. 'Yeah. We had some fun times growing up.'

'My grandmother used to sing me a song to sleep. Not exactly appropriate for a lullaby she said, but it was the only Eurasian song she knew.'

'Really? Let's hear it.'

Gerald taps the time on his thigh with his right hand as his sings:

Jinkli nona, jinkli nona,
Yo kereh casa,
Casa nunteng porta, nona,
Klai logu pasah?

O nona, minya nona,
Qui lonzi bos ta bai,

Si yo nungka tomah con nona,
Nungka filu di mia pai.

O nona, minya nona,
O nona minya korasang,
Si nona muitu bemfeta,
Yo ja kai na a-faesang.

Silence settles as the words and tune expand to fill the space. Martin stirs, as if emerging from a dream. 'What does it mean? My parents only knew the first two lines. Something about a man, he wants to get married …?'

'*Jinkli nona, jinkli nona,* / *Yo kereh casa.* That means "Fair maiden, fair maiden, I want to get married".'

'That part I know.'

'Then it goes on to say the house has no door, so how will they fare?'

'What house?'

'Must be the house they plan to live in lah. Anyway, the second verse is that the maiden has gone far away, and if he doesn't take her for his bride, he's not the son of his father – *nungka filu di mia pai.*'

'Okay.'

'Then the third verse says maiden, maiden of my heart, you are so pretty, I have fallen on my face in love. *Yo jah kai na a-faesang.*'

'Fallen on his face in love? A funny way of putting it.'

'Yeah.'

'How do you remember all that?'

'It's just in here.' He taps his left temple. 'I've heard it so many times. I would sing along with my grandmother. And all these years I keep singing it from time to time, when I'm doing the laundry, on my shift, so I won't forget. But still, sometimes, when I'm singing, I'll realise I'm just making the sounds of the words, I can't recall what they actually mean. I know the gist of it but only when I sit down and think about each line carefully, then it comes back.'

'Don't you have it saved somewhere?'

'Maybe. I can't remember.'

'Could you write it down for me?'

'Of course.' Gerald reaches into his trouser pocket and takes out a writing rod. A thin sheet rolled into a cylinder falls to the ground between them. He stares but makes no move to pick it up. Martin glances at him then reaches down slowly. As he holds it by one corner with his thumb and index finger, it uncurls. An image blooms on the transparent surface. Then Gerald snatches it back and crams it into his pocket.

'That was your wife? She's Filipino?'

'Yes,' comes the terse reply. Then he seems to soften. 'Her parents came here as refugees when the tsunami hit Manila.'

'I see. And who were the two children cutting the birthday cake?'

Gerald contemplates the ash-coloured sky as if watching for real birds. 'Marcus and James.' A heartbeat, then, 'Our twins.'

'You have kids? The census made a mistake?'

'No.' A look of discomfort flits across his face. Martin waits, but the man seems reluctant to elaborate.

He grasps the handle of his walking stick, swishing it through the grass. 'But there are two more of us!'

A rustle behind the bench startles them. A hologram of a deer with translucent red eyes and a creamy pelt wavers behind the trunk of a tree. 'Sambar deer. *Cervus unicolor*. Widely found in Southeast Asia, this species was commonly found in forests. The pale fur and eyes mark an albino,' intones the disembodied voice.

The deer steps away delicately. After it lopes off, the silence hangs heavy. Martin decides not to break it. He wishes he could take back his earlier bluster. Maybe the poor man's sons were dead? Or they'd been adopted? Just as he's decided to change the subject and ask about work, Gerald speaks, his voice flat. 'The census didn't make a mistake. I registered the twins as Filipino.'

'What! I mean – why?'

Gerald takes an age to fold his nut brown hands, with their sheen of moistness, on his lap. His eyes are fixed on them as he talks, as if trying to convince this audience of a particularly stubborn point. 'It was just more practical. Why would I want them to be upset all the time? I spent so much of my life being angry. Angry at feeling invisible, angry that other bloody Singaporeans seemed to think we didn't exist. Yes, there were so few of us, but we still *counted*, goddammit.'

'But what about their surnames? They'd have a Eurasian surname surely, even in a hyphenate?'

Gerald's gaze lifts to the trees. 'Pereira is a common family name in the Philippines.' A pause, then, 'I don't tell them much about being Eurasian.'

Although his eyes are obscured by the reflection of the sky on his spectacles, Martin senses the man's struggle to master dormant emotions.

Eventually, he sucks in a long breath, the tip of his tongue against his front teeth. 'I wanted Marcus and James to focus on other things. I wanted them not to grow up feeling like I did. Bitter. Rootless. I had a chance to make a different life for my kids, without leaving this place.'

'I don't mean to be rude, but – I still can't understand why you didn't just register them as part-Eurasian.'

'What would have been the point? This way, at least they can feel like they have … a lot.'

'A lot of what?'

His tone borders on aggressive. 'Look, I'm a lapsed Catholic, okay? And I can't even remember the last time I ate feng or curry ambilla or what have you, and English is the only thing I speak, plus a bit of Hokkien swear words and the

Malay I scraped from language elective at school.'

Martin measures his response. The last thing he wanted was to alienate the guy. 'Well, I haven't eaten feng in a long time too, and the last time I stepped into any kind of church was on Christmas Eve the first year I got back after I retired. That was an eye-opener. More like an atomic show.'

Gerald makes a kind of snort. 'No, don't you see? I don't have anything *Eurasian* to give them. At least Joyce has a whole bloody country full of culture. Those people have songs, they've got stories, a language, so many dishes their names make my head spin. The boys inherit all that.' Then the agitation suddenly dissolves. His spine seems to go slack. 'Well, they're not boys anymore. They're thirty-two and Marcus has a baby of his own.'

Martin makes the laboured effort to twist his torso to face him.

'My dear friend, you just sang me the whole of *Jinkli Nona*. Of course you have something Eurasian to give them.'

'One song doesn't make a culture.'

Not wanting to make another blithe remark, Martin fusses with his walking stick, then sets it to rest against the exact same spot against the bench. 'I don't think it's sad. If you hadn't bothered to memorise that song all these years, I'd have even less. Shitty as it is, I'm really glad there are two of us and it's not just me.'

Gerald nods absently. 'Another thing my grandmother

told me. They used to classify us as "Others". Can you believe that? You probably already know, but I always thought she was joking till I looked it up one day. But here we are, the two of us. We aren't even "Others" anymore, we're invisible.' He slides his body lower down on the bench and does something that conflates a shrug and a sigh. 'Anyway, come, I'll write it down for you.'

As Martin removes his screen from his trouser pocket, it glows to life. Gerald straightens up, places it on his knee and scribbles. Then he reads over what he's written, flexing the fingers of his right hand. 'God, my handwriting is terrible. It's been a long time man. Well, you can just do that transcribe function.'

Martin accepts the scroll, his eyes running over Gerald's loopy electronic scrawl. 'No. I want to keep it this way. It feels more real.'

They don't speak much after that, but sit back, gazing at the pallid sun hanging behind the veil of gases, enjoying the sweet scent of oxygen-rich air encased in the bubble. It's only when the cycleways become bloated with traffic that they realise the bench has lost its warmth and evening is upon them. Martin likes the fact that dotted in between the solar-powered cycles are the occasional penny-farthings, powered by nothing but human muscle. No doubt, with their riders donning thermoplastic helmets shaped like bowler hats, this was yet another fashion dalliance, but it spoke to him of how some of the young people yearned for a simpler, more honest time.

Gerald interrupts his thoughts. 'Well, Martin, this has been great, but I gotta get back. Dinner with the family.'

'Oh, of course. Don't let me keep you. My dog will be wanting his walk also.' Martin shuffles to his feet, feeling the stiffness in his lower back from having sat in one position for so long.

They shake hands again. Then Gerald massages his left elbow and looks down at his shoes as he speaks. 'This was – we have to do this again.'

'Definitely.'

He lifts his face and the gold flecks in his eyes spark. Martin continues to stand, leaning heavily on his walking stick, as he watches the small man tread down the path out of the dome. The slight figure makes its way onto the pedestrian lane alongside the cycle rush, growing tinier and tinier as it bobs along the undulating ribbon of traffic, until finally it dissolves into the pulsating sweep of humanity.

References and Notes

Introduction

Further reading:

> *Singapore Eurasians: Memories and Hopes* by Ann Ebert-
> Oehlers and Myrna L. Blake
>
> *Eurasians* by Alexius Pereira

The Gift

1. This was originally published in the Spring 2014 issue of *The Wilderness House Literary Review*.

2. Glossary of Kristang terms

gatu bai, gatu beng	the cat goes, the cat comes
buskah ratu	looking for the rat
naki teng	there it is
jah kumi	to have already eaten
cherki jepun	a card game brought to Malacca by Chinese Hokkien traders
yo jah kumi	I have already eaten
yo kumi arus	I eat rice
achar	pickles

tar di nanas	pineapple tarts
farinya	flour
asah kukis	to bake cakes
basiu	plate
glas	glass
agu	water
kuleh	spoon
garfu	fork

Sugee Cake: A (Very Brief) Speculative History

References:

> *The New Food Lover's Companion* by Sharon Tyler Herbst
>
> *Sweet Invention: A History of Dessert* by Michael Krondl

Meeting with the Sea

This was originally published in *Cha: An Asian Literary Review*, June 2016, Issue 32.

The Mosquito

1. My maternal great-grandfather Valentin Sequeira went to Bahau during WWII, and returned to Singapore once during the war, supposedly to buy nails. After he left for Bahau the second time, he never returned. That brief visit to Singapore was the last time his family saw him. The other characters in this story, besides the Sequeiras and Bishop Devals,

are fictional. My grandmother's age in this story has been fictionalised for dramatic purposes.

2. Glossary (Kristang unless stated otherwise)

batu giling	(Malay) a heavy rectangular granite slab with an accompanying granite rolling pin used to grind spices
bong anoti	goodnight
rayu	rascal, naughty
yo jah drumi kon gatu,	I was sleeping with the cat, and it bit
jah murdeh na ku	my bottom

Eurasian Tea is an Actual Thing
References:
> *Tea: A Global History* by Helen Saberi
> *Singapore Eurasians: Memories and Hopes* by Ann Ebert-
>   Oehlers and Myra L. Blake

Blind Date
This was originally published in *LONTAR: Journal of Southeast Asian Speculative Fiction*, #7, October 2016 issue.

Acknowledgements

I'm indebted to my parents, Gwenne Pinto and Oliver De Silva, as well as Kerry Kessler, for contributing their precious oral histories. Also to Nicole Batchelor, who shared her grandmother's lovely teatime tradition. And of course, my own grandmother, dearest Patsy Pinto nee Sequeira, who fed me chocolate rice toast and sang 'Gatu bai, gatu beng', the reason why I began writing this collection.

If you enjoyed this,
you might also like …

You Might Want To Marry My Husband

by Yap Swee Neo

In this intimate collection of autobiographical stories that every woman should read, Swi offers tales of deep reflection that relate to the tears and laughter, and the love and pain felt by girls and women in Malaysia and Singapore over the last 75 years.

Swi recalls the convent sisters in Malacca who educated her and her classmates about sex, the camaraderie among girlfriends, and desires fulfilled. She explores issues of life and death and shares memories of the unforgettable men in her life. Swi holds in high regard the mothers under banana leaf umbrellas who dreamed great dreams for their children, and she introduces us to memorable characters inclduing 'bling, bling, the real thing, Pansy', a lecherous Baba patriarch and his complaining wife, a Jonker Street cake shop baker whose strong arms are made to hug, a Singaporean academic with low EQ, and a nameless Malaysian bondmaid who must secure her place in a wealthy household. These are stories from the heart.